So Long on Lonely Street

by Sandra Deer

SO LONG ON LONELY STREET was originally produced by the Alliance Theatre Company, Atlanta, Georgia. It received its pre-Broadway presentation at the Nickerson Theatre, Norwell, Massachusetts.

D1084525

SAMUEL FRENCH, INC.

45 WEST 25TH STREET   NEW YORK 10010
7623 SUNSET BOULEVARD   HOLLYWOOD 90046
LONDON   *TORONTO*

SO LONG ON LONELY STREET was presented on Broadway by Cheryl Crawford, Paul B. Berkowsky, and Robert Franz, in association with Maxine and Stanford Makover and J. Arnold Nickerson, at the Jack Lawrence Theatre in New York City, on April 3, 1986, with the following cast:

(in order of appearance)

RAYMOND BROWN	Ray Dooley
ANNABEL LEE	Lizan Mitchell
RUTH BROWN	Pat Nesbit
KING VAUGHNUM III	Stephen Root
CLAIRICE VAUGHNUM	Jane Murray
BOBBY STACK	Fritz Sperberg

Directed by KENT STEPHENS

Scenery Designed by Mark Morton
Costumes Designed by Jane Greenwood
Lighting Designed by Allen Lee Hughes

Original Music Composed by Hal Lanier
Production Supervisor — Roger Shea

Originally produced by the Alliance Theatre Company

SO LONG ON LONELY STREET
THE VAUGHNUM FAMILY

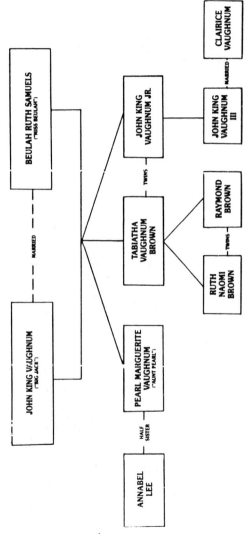

Act One

A late August afternoon at Honeysuckle Hill, a few miles outside a small Southern town.

Act Two (Scene 1)

Later the same evening.

Act Two (Scene 2)

The next morning.

CHARACTERS

RUTH and RAYMOND BROWN — Ruth and Raymond are twins in their late thirties or early forties. They are both attractive, bright, and well educated. Ruth is a poet and Raymond an actor.

ANNABEL LEE — Anna is a black woman, mid-seventies. She has an inner strength, but is not all-wise or long-suffering. She is self-contained and not usually demonstrative.

KING VAUGHNUM III — King is a small town Southern wheeler-dealer. He's around thirty, perhaps a little on the chubby side. Smart, but not a thoughtful man, high energy.

CLAIRICE VAUGHNUM — King's wife. Mid-twenties, seven months pregnant. The kind of woman who is happy and sweet as long as she is the center of attention.

BOBBY STACK — A Southern lawyer, around forty. Polite and sensible. Probably went to University of Virginia Law School.

These are realistic characters, not Southern types. King

is not a buffoon. Clairice is not just a silly twit, and Annabel Lee is nobody's servant. Ruth and Raymond are sophisticated and have traveled, but they are not contemptuous of what they come from.

SET

One set, living room with door leading to unseen kitchen and screened front door going out onto front porch with swing and railing. The sidewalk coming up to the porch is visible. In the living room there is an old upright piano, standard old furniture, a casket, and stairs going up to a visible landing.

So Long on Lonely Street

ACT ONE

As the lights come up, RAYMOND enters up the walk,
onto the porch, and taps on the screen door. He
wears slacks and an expensive sports coat and car-
ries a piece of leather luggage and a bag containing
a bottle of sherry.

SQ 1

SQ 2

RAYMOND. Hello. Annabel Lee. Ruth. Anybody
here? (*sees casket*) Alive?

(*ANNA enters from 2nd story, crosses downstairs.*)

ANNA. I told you all to leave that body alone.
RAYMOND. Miss Anna. It's me. Raymond.
ANNA. Who?
RAYMOND. Raymond.
ANNA. John King?
RAYMOND. No, mam. Raymond. Tabby's boy. Ruth's
brother. I've come home for Aunt Pearl's funeral.
ANNA. Raymond? All the way from New York City?
RAYMOND. That's right. (*crosses to* C. *stage*)
ANNA. Well, how 'bout that. (*They hug.*) Raymond.
Looks like to me your parts are getting smaller.
RAYMOND. My parts?
ANNA. They don't show you every day like they used
to. You used to be one of the main ones.
RAYMOND. (*laughing*) Oh, on "All Our Yesterdays."
Yeah. I'm afraid you're right. Chance Rodney has peaked.
Just a matter of time before old Chance will be the
tragic victim of a brain tumor or a jealous husband.

7

ANNA. You wanna stay here?

RAYMOND. Well, I thought I would if it isn't putting you to any trouble.

ANNA. I mean for good.

RAYMOND. Where's Ruth?

ANNA. You wanna come live here with me and have this place for yourself when I die?

RAYMOND. I don't think so. I just came for Aunt Pearl's funeral. And to see you and Ruth.

ANNA. What's the sense of coming all the way from New York City just to put some old lady in the ground?

RAYMOND. It is a quaint custom, isn't it?

ANNA. How about it? We could fix the place up.

RAYMOND. (*taking the bottle out of the bag and giving it to ANNA*) Could sure use it. This is for you.

ANNA. What is it?

RAYMOND. Sherry. You still like sherry don't you?

ANNA. I still like it.

RAYMOND. (*at phone*) What's Ruth's number?

ANNA. (*occupied with sherry, but not opening it*) She doesn't have one.

RAYMOND. No phone?

ANNA. Doesn't want people pestering her, I guess. You know you shouldn't treat those women so mean.

RAYMOND. What women?

ANNA. Erica DuBois and all those women on your program.

RAYMOND. That's what they pay me for.

ANNA. Shouldn't treat Ruth like that either. Never coming home. Never calling up.

RAYMOND. You just said she doesn't have a telephone.

ANNA. Well she used to.

RAYMOND. Ruth understands why I stay away.

ANNA. She doesn't even watch your program. But I

do. Pearl too. If you was my twin brother, I'd expect to see you sometime. Course, you're not, and you probably don't care what I think. Well let me go get your room ready. (*picks up RAYMOND's coat and bag*)

RAYMOND. Anna, I can do that.

ANNA. I can change the sheets on the beds in my own house.

RAYMOND. (*looking out the window*) The squirrels are at your pecan tree.

ANNA. (*still headed upstairs*) Well, go shoo em off. There's a BB gun in the smoke house. (*RAYMOND crosses to kitchen door. From landing, sticking her head out and shouting:*) Would you rather have Pearl's room? It's got the air conditioner.

SQ 3

RAYMOND. No, mam, my room will be fine. (*exits through kitchen*)

ANNA. It's got the TV too. You want to see your program.

RAYMOND. (*offstage*) No, thanks. I don't watch it.

ANNA. (*to herself*) Don't watch it? If I's on TV, I'd wanta see myself. (*sound of motorcycle*)

RUTH. (*entering, holding motorcycle helmet*) Anna. Annabel Lee.

ANNA. I'm right here. (*crosses downstairs*) No need to wake the dead hollering.

RUTH. Why didn't you call anybody?

ANNA. You want to look at her?

RUTH. Why didn't you tell anybody she'd died?

ANNA. Hadn't gotten around to it. She's still plenty dead to bury.

RUTH. Christ, Anna. You can't just keep a dead body around the house for days. It's unsanitary.

ANNA. Thought you told me one time writers have to look at everything.

RUTH. Experience everything. You don't necessarily have to look at it to experience it.

ANNA. Seems like to me you would, but suit yourself. I don't care whether you look at her or not. She was an ugly old bitch when she was alive, and she's an ugly old bitch now.

RUTH. How'd you get her down here?

ANNA. I let the undertaker do that. But that's all he's doing. Pearl wouldn't a liked men messing with her body.

RUTH. Are you alright?

ANNA. Course I am. Dying ain't contagious. Can you open this?

RUTH. Amontillado. How fitting.

ANNA. It's sherry. (*crosses to cabinet, gets two sherry glasses*)

RUTH. *The Cask of Amontillado.* It's a story. A man gets sealed up in a wine cellar. Alive.

ANNA. Hmmm. Does he die?

RUTH. It's not about dying. It's about being buried alive.

ANNA. Wonder what that's like. Being buried alive. Hmmm. Guess I'll be good and dead when they bury me.

RUTH. Well, give us a call before you kick off, so you won't end up lying around the house a week before anybody knows you're dead.

ANNA. Won't have to. You'll be living here.

RUTH. Like hell I will. I'll never live in this house again. (*lights cigarette*)

ANNA. You remember that man, that doctor in South Carolina wrote a book about the woman was more than one person inside of her?

RUTH. *The Three Faces of Eve?*

ANNA. That's the one. Well, I'm like that. You come

live here and watch me all the time and write a book about me and Sharon Rose. *The Two Faces of Anna.* You can keep all the money.

RUTH. You old fraud. You don't have a split personality. You made Sharon Rose up to get attention.

ANNA. That is a lie. Sharon Rose is a real person. She lives inside my head just like Eve. Sometimes she pushes the rest of me right out of the way. You could make a lot of money writing a book about her and me. You are sitting on a gold mine.

RUTH. Annabel Lee, you have been trotting out that Sharon Rose character for as long as I can remember. You made her up, like an imaginary playmate. You may be crazy, but you are not clinically interesting.

ANNA. Sharon Rose is the daughter of King Solomon.

RUTH. Anna.

ANNA. All right, all right. Maybe I did make her up at first. But not to get attention. And not to have somebody to play with. I made her up to have somebody to be.

RUTH. What's wrong with being Annabel Lee?

ANNA. And who would that be? Who the hell is Annabel Lee? Huh? A little colored girl growing up and growing old in the middle of a rich white family. Eating with them, playing with their toys, wearing their clothes. But not being one of them. No way I could ever be one of them. Wasn't one of anything. A freak. That's Annabel Lee. A freak.

RUTH. Anna, I thought . . .

ANNA. You could write a book about that. People like hearing about freaks.

RUTH. You've always been treated like one of the family.

ANNA. No such thing as *like* one of the family, Ruth. Either you are, or you're not. You are, and I'm not.

RUTH. That's ridiculous. You are . . .

ANNA. You want to write a book about me?

RUTH. Anna, I have a job.

ANNA. Huh. Teaching poem writing to a bunch of pimply-faced rednecks. How much they pay over at that Junior College? (*sound of BB gun from outside*)

RUTH. What was that?

ANNA. A BB gun. Damned squirrels are going to get every pecan I've got.

RAYMOND. (*offstage; from off, probably the kitchen*) Anna, where's my motorcycle? (*entering*) It was in the smoke house, but it's . . . Hello, Ruthie.

RUTH. Raymond. (*Big hug; then break away and look at each other. To ANNA:*) Why didn't you tell me he was here?

ANNA. I'm trying to talk business with you. (*to RAY-MOND*) You get any of em?

RAYMOND. (*eyes only for RUTH*) No, mam, I just scared them away. (*to RUTH*) How are you?

ANNA. Scare them away. They're gonna come right back. (*gets 3rd sherry glass*)

RUTH. (*without anger*) I shouldn't even be speaking to you.

RAYMOND. What did I do?

ANNA. I know what's in the will.

RUTH. Nothing. Five years. That's what you did. Five years and not a letter, not a phone call.

RAYMOND. I'm here now.

ANNA. You hear what I said? I know what's in the will.

RAYMOND. What will? You look wonderful.

RUTH. You look good too.

ANNA. Your grandaddy's will. Knew Pearl had it hid around here somewhere. Took me two days to find it. Know where she had it hid?

RAYMOND. Thanks. Had what hid?

ANNA. The will. Your grandaddy's will.

RAYMOND. Where?

ANNA. (*moving towards the trunk*) In that old trunk full of your mama's things.

RUTH. So that's why you hadn't gotten around to calling the undertaker. Pearl's lying up there dead while you ransack the house for her will.

ANNA. Wasn't in the house. Was in the smoke house. I had to know what was in it before King did. He thinks I'm crazy. (*gives sherry to RAYMOND*)

RAYMOND. Did you see my motorcycle in the smoke house?

RUTH. Come outside with me.

RAYMOND. What for?

ANNA. King's after the property, but it's mine.

RAYMOND. Is that what the will says?

ANNA. You bet it does. All mine. The house and the land.

RUTH. (*glancing around*) Congratulations. Come on, Raymond.

ANNA. Listen, Ruth. You think it's smart to act like you're too good to care about owning things. When you get older you'll find out. Property and money is the only things between you and the poor house or snooty people's charity.

RUTH. Right. Come on, Raymond.

ANNA. Wait a minute. I'm talking about property. You gonna let me finish or not.

RUTH. Yes m'am.

ANNA. It won't take long. Now sit down and let me finish. The will says when I die, the places goes to the cousins. You two and King. Unless one of you wants to live here. That's the way Big Jack left it. You live here with me, the place is yours when I die. And that won't be too long.

RAYMOND. If the place is yours, what difference does it make who gets it when you die? What do you care whether it goes to Ruth or all three of us together?

ANNA. I don't. Don't care a bit. Can go to the devil for all I care. You want it?

RAYMOND. No, I don't . . .

ANNA. Then it's got to be Ruth. If one of you's not living here with me, King'll tell 'em I'm crazy and not fit to live here by myself on my property. If Ruth's living here with me, it won't matter whether I'm crazy or not.

RAYMOND. Makes sense. It wouldn't hurt you to have it, Ruth.

RUTH. It's been hurting me all my life.

ANNA. But it didn't belong to you all your life. Property can only hurt you when it's somebody else's. King means to get this land. All the time Pearl was sick, he'd come over and sit and hold her hand and try to sweet talk her into leaving it to him.

RAYMOND. He didn't know it wasn't hers to leave?

ANNA. Nope. And she didn't tell him either. She'd just lie there and smile and try to look like an angel on her way to heaven and let him keep on sweet talking. Pearl's favorite thing was to have people begging her. She never gave nobody nothing, unless she'd got tired of it. But she'd make you think she was going to so you'd keep on asking. One time when we was little, Big Jack gave her a puppy. He said, "Now you let Anna play with him too." But he gave it to her. I'd say, "Pearl, let me hold him. I'll give him right back." And she'd say, "In a minute. You can hold him in a minute." She named him Dusty. She'd rub his fur and talk babytalk to him. Everytime I'd ask her to hold him, she'd say, "In a minute, Anna. I'll let you hold Dusty in a minute. We sat out there on the steps all morning with Pearl petting her puppy and me begging to hold him. I wanted to hold that puppy so bad I was almost crying. And she just kept saying, "In a minute, Anna. In a minute." Miss Beulah must have been sitting in here listening to us fussing all that time. Cause after awhile she came out on the porch and she was furious. I never seen her mad like that. She said, "Pearl, let Anna hold that puppy." And Pearl said, "I will in a minute, Mama. Daddy gave him to me." And Miss Beulah nelly went wild. She said, "I don't care what your daddy did. You let Anna hold that puppy now, or I'll tell Nathan to take him down to the pond and drown him." Pearl turned around and said, "Here!" and threw the puppy at me. If I hadn't a caught him, it would have bashed his brains out on that concrete step. She could be so hateful.

RAYMOND. Anna, you know we'll take care of you. Whatever happens about the house, Ruth and I . . .

ANNA. That Dusty. Cute lil' ole puppy. Turned out to be one of the meanest, ugliest old hounds we ever had.

RUTH. All these years you and Pearl lived together like sisters, and you never felt . . .

ANNA. We didn't live together *like* sisters. We *were* sisters. Half sisters, anyway. I expect you already knew that, didn't you? (*pause*) Well, didn't you?

RAYMOND. We heard things when we were children. But we never . . .

ANNA. Course you did.

RAYMOND. If you knew, why didn't you ever say anything?

ANNA. No reason to til now. Wasn't something I was proud of.

RUTH. Did Big Jack tell you?

ANNA. Huh. He never told me nothing. When I's little I never thought about why I's here or who I belonged to. Never remembered being anywhere else. One day when I was six or seven, Nathan's mama, Sarah, was gon' take him and his sisters to the camp meeting. I asked him if I could go too and he said I could. I waited all afternoon for him to come get me, but he never did. Next day, I asked him why. Said his mama said she couldn't take me 'cause I's Big Jack's little girl, and he wouldn't like it. Me going with the colored. First time I really thought about it. Being colored and being here.

RAYMOND. And you never asked him who your mother was or why you were brought here? You never even told him you knew?

ANNA. No. But I'm telling now. I've outlived 'em all, and this place is going to be mine. What's left of it. Unless King finds a way to get me off of it. If Ruth's living with me, he can't. He can't get rid of both of us.

RUTH. I can't, Anna. This place and this family has screwed me up all my life. I'm not going to come back here and . . .

ANNA. You could think about it.

RUTH. Raymond, you want to go down to the pond?

RAYMOND. (*following RUTH toward the door*) She'll think about it. (*coming out on the porch*) Hey, that's my motorcycle.

RUTH. I drug it out of the smokehouse and cleaned it up.

ANNA. Will you think about it?

RAYMOND. My Harley Davidson.   SQ 4

RUTH. Well, get on.

RAYMOND. My youth.

ANNA. You could. You don't want to. (*ANNA moves to the casket, looks in, and sings.*)

Pretty little Pearl
Pretty little Pearl.
Looks like an angel . . .
How's it feel being dead? You like it? (*Sound of a car*   SQ 5
outside.) Here they come. Both of 'em. Don't let 'em
talk you to death.

(*ANNA exits upstairs. KING and CLAIRICE enter
    talking. He carries a funeral parlor stand with a
    light on it, and she carries a guest book.*)

CLAIRICE. Does it smell?
KING. It was starting to just a little, but I aired it out.
Now, don't look at her.
CLAIRICE. Has she turned black and stiff?
KING. She hadn't been dead but a few days. She looks
'bout like she always did. Only more. (*crosses left,
places stand near coffin*)
CLAIRICE. Seems like to me a body would start to
decompose pretty quick in the middle of August.
KING. Not when the air conditioner in her room is
running full blast twenty-four hours a day. I hate to
think what that utility bill is going to look like. You got
the book?
CLAIRICE. Here.
KING. (*bending down behind a table to reach the
outlet*) Wait a minute. Let me get the thing plugged in.
CLAIRICE. Well, you asked me for it. You know I
can't believe it. I still cannot believe it.
KING. Everybody dies sooner or later, Clairice. She
was seventy-four years old.
CLAIRICE. I don't mean Aunt Pearl dying. I mean that
crazy old Negress keeping her body up there for three
days and not telling anybody.

KING. Shhh. Don't call her a crazy old Negress.

CLAIRICE. Well, what do you want me to call her?

KING. Nothing. I want you to be nice to her. The last thing I need is trouble from Annabel Lee.

CLAIRICE. Well, if that's what you consider acceptable behavior, for somebody to just keep a dead body in the house like it was sleeping. I think it is grotesque. If you hadn't come over here to see Pearl, there's no telling how long her body would have stayed up there. We'd probably have to have the whole house fumigated.

ANNA. (*offstage; voice as SHARON ROSE from upstairs*) I am the Rose of Sharon. The lily of the valley.

CLAIRICE. Hear that? And you tell me she's not crazy.

KING. I didn't say she wasn't crazy. I said for you not to call her crazy. For God's sake, Clairice . . . (*CLAIRICE glances into the casket and sees Pearl's body. She screams.*)

CLAIRICE. Aiii.

KING. Dammit, I told you not to look at her.

CLAIRICE. What's the matter with her?

KING. Miss Anna wouldn't let the undertaker touch her. Said she'd be buried like she was or not at all.

CLAIRICE. But she looks hideous. Who does Miss Anna think she is bossing everybody around like that? It's not her place to say how we treat the body of a member of your family, is it? Well, is it?

(*BOBBY STACK comes up on the front porch and knocks.*)

KING. Well, hey there, Bobby. How you doing?

BOBBY. Well as can be expected, I guess. Afternoon, Clairice. How's old Roy doing?

CLAIRICE. He's just fine. You know he's gone back to

Jessup and gone to work in Daddy's tire store.

BOBBY. Is that a fact. Well good for him. 'Bout time he settled down. (*to KING*) You know, back in college that brother of hers could out cuss a sailor and drink any man . . .

CLAIRICE. Well, Roy's changed now, Bobby. That was a long time ago.

BOBBY. Boy, I'll say. Longer than I like to remember. Well, the reason I came over, I just wanted to pay my respects and tell you how sorry I was to hear about your aunt.

KING. Thank you, Bobby.

BOBBY. Guess Ruth'll be coming over from Sparta today?

CLAIRICE. (*to KING*) Don't let him see what she looks like.

KING. (*getting between BOBBY and the casket as BOBBY moves to sign the book*) Yeah. Ruth oughta be here pretty soon. You oughta get that girl to marry you, fella. She could use some settling down.

BOBBY. What you think I been trying to do? Your cousin doesn't seem to have much use for country lawyers.

KING. Sure she does. Sure she does. You just gotta hang in there. (*closes coffin lid*)

BOBBY. Well, she don't seem to have much use for me. I thought maybe she'd be here by now.

KING. For some reason unbeknownst to me, cousin Ruth has had her phone disconnected. I sent one of my taxi cab drivers over to Sparta with a note telling her about Aunt Pearl.

CLAIRICE. And King called New York City long distance to tell Ruth's brother Raymond, who is, as you may know, Chance Rodney, one of the main stars on "All Our Yesterdays." King actually talked to Chance

Rodney in person on the telephone.

KING. Well, not exactly in person. I talked to a tape recording of his voice. I told it . . .eh him, Aunt Pearl had died and that the funeral was tomorrow and to get hisself on down here.

CLAIRICE. We're going to have him over to our house for supper tonight if he gets here in time. Aren't we, King.

KING. Eh, Bobby, about the estate, settling it, I mean. There aren't gonna be any problems 'bout that are there?

BOBBY. I don't foresee any. It's a little complicated, but nothing that can't be worked out.

KING. Complicated how? It goes to the grandchildren, don't it? What's complicated about that?

BOBBY. Well, I'm really not at liberty to discuss it with you right now, King. Soon as I get together with the executor and decide . . .

KING. Executor. What executor?

BOBBY. Well, the oldest living grandchild's the executor.

KING. The oldest? Why the oldest? I'm the one that's here.

BOBBY. I have to follow my instructions. Which one's the oldest, Ruth or Raymond?

CLAIRICE. They're twins.

BOBBY. I know, but one of them had to be born first. Which ever one it was, that's who's the executor. Or executrix if it's Ruth.

KING. Ruth! Jesus Christ. Not Ruth.

CLAIRICE. King.

BOBBY. Well, I better be going. We oughta set a time in the next couple of weeks to discuss the estate. It affects you and Ruth and Raymond and Annabel Lee.

KING. Annabel Lee? What's she got to do with

anything?

BOBBY. (*starting to leave*) She's in it.

KING. Eh, Bobby, wait a minute. Listen, why don't we just go ahead and read the will right away. Why don't we just go ahead and read it tomorrow?

BOBBY. I thought the funeral was tomorrow.

KING. In the afternoon. We could meet right here and read the will first thing and get all this estate business out of the way before we go out to the cemetery.

BOBBY. I don't know, King. That seems awful soon. People usually . . . Well, I guess if that's what everybody wants to do, no reason why . . .

KING. Good. That's fine. Then we'll see you here tomorrow. 'Bout noontime?

BOBBY. Okay. Tell Ruth I'll see her then.

KING. I'm sure she'll be looking forward to seeing you. (*BOBBY exits front door and out.*) Damn that old woman. She coulda told me.

CLAIRICE. What does he mean about complications? SQ 6

KING. It don't change anything. Still just a matter of buying Ruth and Raymond out.

CLAIRICE. And Annabel Lee. Don't forget about her.

KING. Her too. If I have to. Everything's fine. Just take a little longer.

CLAIRICE. But what about your partners? You said you had to . . .

KING. I told you everything's fine. (*Door heard closing upstairs.*) That's Miss Anna. Now you be polite to her, hear. She'll be gone soon enough.

CLAIRICE. Not soon enough to suit me.

KING. Clairice!

CLAIRICE. Of course, I'll be polite.

(*ANNA comes down the stairs. She pauses at the landing and looks at the stand next to the casket.*)

KING. Hey there, Miss Anna. Bobby Stack was just here. You just this minute missed him.

ANNA. What's that?

KING. Why, it's Aunt Pearl.

ANNA. Not in the casket. That thing next to it.

CLAIRICE. That is the book where people are supposed to sign when they come to pay their respects. Mr. Sammons' boy refused to come back in this house after the way you acted. So King had to bring it over himself.

ANNA. Nobody's coming. Get that thing outa here.

CLAIRICE. Miss Anna, the Vaughnums are a very important family. Naturally people in the community are going to want to come by and . . .

ANNA. I already told that undertaker, and I told the preacher. I don't want nobody coming here gaping at Pearl and bringing their damn pound cakes.

CLAIRICE. (*grasping her stomach*) Please do not swear in front of my baby.

KING. Clairice, you stay calm. Miss Anna, there's no need to . . .

ANNA. I gave nobody permission to put a funeral parlor stand in this house.

CLAIRICE. Well, it is not your house, you know.

KING. All right, I'll take it out. Just don't shout. And don't get Clairice upset. (*ANNA starts pulling the stand.*) I'll do that, Miss Anna. If you'll just wait a minute. You have to unplug the light first. (*The cord pulls out of the wall as ANNA drags the stand toward the door. The socket fizzles. ANNA keeps going as KING talks.*) We'll have to pay Sammons for that, Miss Anna.

ANNA. Call 'em up and tell 'em to come get their stand.

CLAIRICE. Annabel Lee, I think you should know,

King went to a lot of trouble to make all these arrangements. It looks to me like you could show a little appreciation instead of . . . (*ANNA is at the phone starting to dial.*)

KING. (*taking the phone from her and hanging it up*) I said I'd take care of it. We came over here to comfort you, goddammit. It's proper that we all be together to share our grief over the loss of Aunt Pearl.

ANNA. I don't want to share your grief, and I hadn't lost nothing 'cept a selfish white girl who looked at me everyday for seventy years and thought to herself that the only thing worse than being her would be being me.

KING. Miss Anna! She was your life-long companion. She loved you.

ANNA. She loved her misery. And she considered me part of it. (*exits to kitchen*)

CLAIRICE. Did you know King called Raymond in New York City? He'll probably be here by tonight.

ANNA. (*offstage*) Already got here.

CLAIRICE. He did? Oh my goodness. Did you hear that, King? He's already here. Does he look like he does on "All Our Yesterdays"? (*takes compact out of purse*)

KING. Guess he's just as funny looking as he always was.

CLAIRICE. Funny looking. Not hardly.

KING. Kinda prissy looking if you ask me.

CLAIRICE. Huh. He has charisma. He'll do the meanest things to those women on "All Our Yesterdays," and they just keep coming right back and falling in love with him. I wish Raymond would bring his little girl to see us sometime.

KING. Last I heard, his ex-wife had taken little Heather and moved to Chicago. (*sits on sofa*)

ANNA. What's Heather?

KING. Raymond's little girl.

ANNA. What kind of name is that?

KING. American, I guess.

CLAIRICE. I think it's a real pretty name. I like modern names like that. Don't you like that name, King? (*As CLAIRICE is talking, ANNA has moved to the dictionary at the bookcase, is leafing through it, oblivious of their conversation.*)

KING. Well, sure, but I'm not giving up on this baby being named John King Vaughnum the fourth.

CLAIRICE. Well, that would suit me just fine too. You better believe it would. Then I'd have my big King and my little King. But if it's a girl, don't you think Heather has a nice sound? It's so feminine it's . . . (*ANNA reading to herself from the dictionary.*)

ANNA. A shrub.

CLAIRICE. What's that, Miss Anna?

ANNA. (*reading*) A low growing purplish shrub. That's what heather is. Raymond's girl is named after a bush.

CLAIRICE. Well, it's not the meaning of the word so much. It's the pretty sound.

ANNA. Don't matter how pretty it sounds. Manure. That's a pretty sounding word. Means cowshit. Heather means bush.

CLAIRICE. Miss Anna, you are just hopeless.   SQ 7

ANNA. Not yet.

CLAIRICE. King and I, we just want to do what's best for you.

ANNA. (*moving to the stand again*) Then get this damn thing out of my house.

KING. (*trying to get it away from her*) I will. I said I would. Will you just hold your horses a minute. (*sound of motorcycle arriving offstage*)

CLAIRICE. (*looking out the window*) Oh dear Lord, it's him. King, do I look all right? (*RUTH and RAYMOND enter up the walk. ANNA exits to kitchen.*)

KING. You look fine. (*louder*) Well, well, the prodigal son returns. Somebody go fry us up a mess of fatted calf. How are you, Ray boy? Long time no see. (*shaking hands*) How's things in the movie star business?

CLAIRICE. King.

KING. Huh? Oh, Raymond, meet my wife, Clairice. Honey, this is my cousin Raymond Brown, alias Chance Rodney.

CLAIRICE. How do you do, Raymond. Or should I say, Chance?

RAYMOND. (*taking her hand*) Raymond's fine. How do you do, Clairice.

CLAIRICE. (*almost beside herself*) Just look at those eyes. You have just as much charisma up close as you do on TV.

RAYMOND. Well thank you. That's the name of the game, I guess. Charisma.

CLAIRICE. I can certainly understand why Erica DuBois can't keep her hands off you.

KING. Clairice, it's just a television program. It ain't real life.

RAYMOND. (*moving to the stand*) Are we fighting over the furniture already?

KING. I took the liberty of making all the arrangements. Somebody had to. And, as is their normal procedure, and perfectly appropriate, Mr. Sammons sent over this stand so our friends could sign the book when they come to pay their respects.

RAYMOND. What friends?

CLAIRICE. For your information, Bobby Stack was already here. Did you know him, Raymond? He is one of the most prominent young lawyers in the county. You could do a lot worse, Ruth.

RUTH. (*stands behind the stand*) Friends, we are gathered here today to pay final tribute to the oldest virgin in Bartow County.

CLAIRICE. (*to KING*) Are you going to let her desecrate the memory of your favorite aunt? And in front of our guest?

RUTH. Now, Clairice, let's give credit where credit is due. If there is any man here, who can bear witness that Pearl Marguerite Vaughnum did not die with her maidenhead rigidly intact, let him . . .

KING. Ruth, are you going to start already?

RUTH. You're supposed to pay tribute to the dead. (*sits on sofa*) What else is there to say about Aunt Pearl? I think that's something of a distinction. To die a virgin at seventy-four. (*RAYMOND sits on sofa.*)

CLAIRICE. I didn't realize that you were among those of us who considered virginity an essential virtue for a woman.

RUTH. (*looking at CLAIRICE's stomach*) Why, Clairice, are you still a virgin?

KING. Now look here. There's somebody dead here. Now is not the time for us to be fighting and getting each other mad.

RUTH. I'm not mad. Raymond's not mad.

RAYMOND. I just got here. (*ANNA re-enters.*)

RUTH. Are you mad, Anna?

ANNA. I'll be fine when that funeral parlor stand is off my property. (*KING picks the stand up in disgust and takes it outside, off porch.*)

KING. There. Are you satisfied?

CLAIRICE. Ruth, I want you to know that I have love in my heart for you.

RAYMOND. (*up*) Anna, could I have something to drink?

KING. That's a fantastic idea. I bet Ray could use a nice glass of iced tea after his motorcycle ride. How 'bout that, Miss Anna? (*ANNA starts toward the kitchen.*)

RAYMOND. I'll help you, Anna. You like the lemon sliced in nice thin circles, right?

CLAIRICE. I'll be glad to do that, Raymond.

ANNA. (*still headed to the kitchen with RAYMOND following her*) Raymond can help me. You got a good memory, honey. She cuts the lemon in those ugly little wedges.

RUTH. (*following ANNA and RAYMOND in the kitchen*) No iced tea for me. I prefer some of the vodka King keeps hidden in the sideboard.

CLAIRICE. Vodka. What does she mean, King? You promised me . . .

KING. She doesn't mean anything. Don't you see, she's just trying to stir up trouble. Now, Honey, I think I better remind you how important it is for everybody to get along right now. All my plans depend on getting this property free and clear before September first. This is the beginning of my vision. And we don't want to get anybody riled up, do we?

CLAIRICE. I know all that. And I am not getting anybody riled up. I'm the one that's riled up. Having to listen to Annabel Lee be so ungrateful and Ruth acting so hateful. And vulgar. In front of him.

KING. Clairice, it don't matter. Let 'em act however they want to. Just be nice. Now will you promise me that? Whatever they do, you be nice?

CLAIRICE. Ruth's the one you oughta be telling to be nice.

KING. You are missing the point here.

RUTH. (*enters with a glass in her hand*) What point is that, King?

KING. The point that we are all family. That's the point, isn't it? And at a time like this we oughta be acting like family.

CLAIRICE. Annabel Lee is not actually family. I mean, in a manner of speaking she may be. But actually she isn't part of the official Vaughnum family. I mean obviously she isn't.

RUTH. Well, actually, she is. I mean not obviously, but actually. She is.

CLAIRICE. What do you mean?

KING. Now we don't know that for a fact, Ruth.

RUTH. No, but we know it for the truth.

CLAIRICE. What are y'all talking about?

KING. Nothing, Honey. Ruth's just referring to . . .

RUTH. We are talking about the fact that Annabel Lee is the bastard daughter of our beloved grandfather, Big Jack Vaughnum.

CLAIRICE. (*shocked*) What?

KING. We do not know that to be a fact, and even if she is . . .

RUTH. Everybody's known it for years. Big Jack got away with it, because back then everybody in the county either worked for him or owed him money.

CLAIRICE. I don't believe it. Big Jack loved Miss Beulah. (*to KING*) You told me how much he loved Miss Beulah. And how after she died, everyday for the rest of his life he'd drive by the cemetery at lunchtime and toot the horn and say, "Hey there, Miss Beulah, I'll be coming to join you pretty soon."

KING. Course he loved Miss Beulah. She was a saint. Everybody loved her. But Big Jack, well, Honey, he was a man with a lot of strong needs, and a lady like Miss Beulah . . .

CLAIRICE. Are you saying it's true?

KING. Well, it don't really matter that much, does it? It was seventy-five years ago.

CLAIRICE. Of course it matters. It . . . (*ANNA and RAYMOND enter with a tray of iced tea.*)

KING. My goodness that looks delicious. And fresh mint too. Miss Anna, you are the hostess with the mostess. Here, Honey, have a nice cold glass of Anna's iced tea. This kind of weather, nothing like a good glass of iced tea to hit the spot. Isn't that right, Raymond?

RAYMOND. You bet.

RUTH. Is there anything more you'd like to say about the tea? How about you, Clairice. Is your iced tea refreshing and delicious?

CLAIRICE. It's just fine.

KING. You bet it is. Best tea in Bartow County. Where you going? (*ANNA is exiting upstairs.*)

ANNA. Time for my nap.

CLAIRICE. King, I need to go home.

KING. What's the matter, Honey? Is it the . . .

CLAIRICE. I just need to lie down.

KING. You want to lie down here? We could take you upstairs and . . .

CLAIRICE. I don't want to lie down here. I want to go home.

KING. But I need to talk to Ruth and Raymond. I need to . . . Okay. Okay. Here, let me help you to the car. You feel faint, Honey? You think we oughta go to the hospital?

CLAIRICE. Just take me home.

KING. (*as he and CLAIRICE are exiting*) Okay. That's where we're going. Right now. Uh, I'll be right

back, y'all. I'm just gonna take Clairice home to lie
down a little while.

RAYMOND. King sure picked himself a ripe little SQ 8
peach.

RUTH. She's one of your biggest fans.

RAYMOND. Woman knows charisma when she sees it.

RUTH. You don't have to wait for somebody to die to
come home, you know.

RAYMOND. Somebody always does. I've missed you.
(*sits on sofa*)

RUTH. How long can you stay?

RAYMOND. Til tomorrow night.

RUTH. Tomorrow night! (*crosses stage* R.)

RAYMOND. I've got to be back in New York Thursday.
Life goes on.

RUTH. Doesn't it. What is she this time? Writer? Pro-
ducer? Not another actress . . .

RAYMOND. No. Actually, she's a student.

RUTH. A student? You mean a graduate student?

RAYMOND. Eh, no. Just a regular student. College.

RUTH. How old is she? (*sits on sofa*)

RAYMOND. She's very precocious.

RUTH. No doubt. How old?

RAYMOND. Twenty.

RUTH. Twenty! Twenty! These blue jeans are older
than that.

RAYMOND. It's nothing serious. Right now I'm here to
see you.

RUTH. No you're not. You're here for Pearl's funeral.

RAYMOND. Well, that's the occasion, not the reason.
You know that.

RUTH. You never write. (*up*)

RAYMOND. I send you postcards and presents. I don't
know what to say to you in a letter.

RUTH. We're running out of people to die, brother. Once Anna's gone there won't be any reason for you to come home. Then we'll be down to just us. (*exits front door, crosses to porch, RAYMOND follows*)

RAYMOND. What about Anna? Is she all right?

RUTH. Slightly batty. She thinks she's nothing.

RAYMOND. Annabel Lee? Ha! She's something. God knows what, but she's definitely something.

RUTH. That's what I thought too, but she claims being brought up in a white family left her with no self-image.

RAYMOND. She didn't say that.

RUTH. Not those words, but that's what she meant.

RAYMOND. She's got more self-image than all the rest of us put together. (*He recites from memory something he and RUTH have heard ANNA say all their lives. RUTH helps in a couple of places he doesn't remember.*) Pearl is a jewel, but I am a poem. Miss Beulah taught me the poem that I am.
It was many and many a year ago,
In a kingdom by the sea.
That a maiden there lived whom you may know
By the name of Annabel Lee;

And this maiden she lived with no other thought
Then to love and be loved by me.

I was a child and she was a child,
In this kingdom by the sea,

But we loved with a love that was more than love
I and my . . .

RUTH. How's your daughter?

RAYMOND. I don't see her much now they aren't in New York.

RUTH. But you send her postcards. And presents.

RAYMOND. Yes.

RUTH. Sorry about your wife. About the divorce, I mean.

RAYMOND. I wasn't meant to be married anymore than you were.

RUTH. Don't be too sure about me, kiddo. Maybe I'll marry Bobby Stack.

RAYMOND. Bobby Stack! Is he still mooning after you?

RUTH. Indeed he is. Passionately.

RAYMOND. Ruth, you could have him for breakfast.

RUTH. I have.

RAYMOND. Not old Bobby.

RUTH. He wants to take care of me.

RAYMOND. Do you need taking care of?

RUTH. Couldn't hurt. And Bobby's rich and respectable . . .

RAYMOND. Respectable! As I recall, Ruth Naomi Brown was what nice people referred to as "wild."

RUTH. When we were young I was wild. Then I got older. I was just promiscuous.

RAYMOND. Was?

RUTH. Sleeping my way across Europe was fine, but after I moved back here, it seemed sort of tacky. I used to think I'd end up killing myself like Mama.

RAYMOND. Ruth, we are not like Mother and Uncle John King.

RUTH. We're twins just like them.

RAYMOND. We're like each other. That doesn't mean we have to be like our mother and her twin.

RUTH. You don't think so? Anyway, when I decided to stop being "wild," I also decided to stop thinking of suicide on a regular basis. Things come in quirky pairs, don't they?

RAYMOND. Like you and me.

RUTH. You and me. I and thou. A quirky pair indeed.

RAYMOND. Anna says you don't watch my show.

RUTH. I did a couple of times.

RAYMOND. Oh. (*pause*) Didn't care for it?

RUTH. It was alright.

RAYMOND. Not your cup of tea.

RUTH. You don't have to apologize to me for what you do. It's a respectable living isn't it?

RAYMOND. There's that word again.

RUTH. You know you're lucky, nobody gives a damn where an actor comes from. Writers it's different. If you were born in the South, you are Southern forever, and God help you if you aren't Gothic.

RAYMOND. You're speaking as a Southern poet in residence now, I take it.

RUTH. Right. But I'm getting better at being Gothic. I may turn into one of those old maids who reads the *National Enquirer* and keeps cats.

RAYMOND. Or marry some pompous assed lawyer whose idea of passion is getting his hand inside your panty girdle. If you hit me I'll hit you back. (*tussle*)

KING. (*coming up the sidewalk*) Here I am. Just like I promised. Boy it's not easy being an expectant father. Ray, I sure am sorry it has to be such a sad and tragic occasion that reunites us. We three's all that's left of the Vaughnum family now, you know. Till my boy is born, I mean.

RUTH. Raymond has a daughter, King.

KING. Course he does. Little Heather. But she lives with her mother and her stepdaddy now I understand. Ruthie, get me a glass of iced tea, please. (*RUTH stares at him and does not move.*) Honey, I'm mighty hot and thirsty.

RUTH. You know where the kitchen is.

KING. Now, Ruthie, I know you don't mean that. You wasn't brought up to . . .

RAYMOND. I think she does, King. We were both brought up to be contrary as old mules.

KING. So's I. So's I. We come by it naturally, don't we. Big Jack used to say when Miss Beulah got in one of her stubborn moods, she wouldn't say gee or haw. Wouldn't say gee or haw. I told that story to Clairice one time, and she didn't know what I was talking about. I said, "Well, Honey, that's what you say to mules when you're plowing. You want 'em to turn this a way, you say gee. You want 'em to turn the other way, you say haw." Clairice said she wasn't brought up to talk to mules. But we was, wasn't we, cousin? We come from the land, and we know the feel of a plow in the hand and the good ole smell of turned up earth. Vaughnum earth.

RUTH. King, you never followed a plow in your life.

KING. It's my heritage. And I am a man who puts great stock in his heritage. Memory is the only thing that separates us from the animals.

RAYMOND. Well, I seem to remember that Big Jack got rid of all the mules and plows before Ruth and I started first grade. By the time you were born all the mules had been replaced by Allis Chalmers. Why your heritage ain't mules and plows, King boy. Your heritage is tractors.

RUTH. King doesn't drive.

KING. Well, I know how to drive. Cars or tractors, and I know when I'm being made fun of. I know you two went off to college and traveled all over and got smart and think you're better than everybody. But there's more important things to do in life than write poems and priss around on TV. I'm the one that's made something of hisself. I'm the one that's gonna lead this family out of its land of famine. So if you want to make your little jokes at my expense, just go right ahead. It won't hurt my feelings one bit.

RAYMOND. I think we owe King an apology. If Ruth and I have indulged ourselves at your expense in the past, we're sorry, aren't we, Ruth? I think we should forget about the past. Except the part that's our heritage, of course, and look toward the future. I say let's give it another shot, King boy. How 'bout it, Ruth?

RUTH. (*starting into the house*) I think I'll just have another shot.

KING. (*heading in the house*) That's a good idea. I got some family business to talk over with both of you, and a nice highball be just the ticket to help us all relax. You just sit still, Ruth. I'll get it. Eh, I didn't exactly mean what I said about you being on TV, Ray. You've done real well for yourself and we're all mighty proud of you. (*He exits into kitchen. RUTH sits on sofa.*)

RAYMOND. (*calling after him*) None for me, thanks.

RUTH. Why don't you priss on over here and sit next to me?

RAYMOND. Why doesn't he drive? (*sits on sofa*)

RUTH. He ran up on a sidewalk and hit an old lady a few years ago. Drunk.

RAYMOND. Hurt her badly?

RUTH. Killed her. Scared him to death. If he weren't John King Vaughnum the third, our cousin would probably be in the penitentiary right now.

RAYMOND. What's he want to talk to us about?

RUTH. I don't know, but I wish you'd stop playing this good old boy game with him.

RAYMOND. Why, Honey, King and me, we're the Southern planters in residence.

RUTH. Please.

RAYMOND. Too gothic for you? (*KING returns with a tray with glasses and a bag of potato chips.*)

KING. Here we are. Ruth. And here you are, Raymond.

RAYMOND. No, King, I don't care for a highball just now.

KING. Aw, come on. Just one little one.

RAYMOND. No. Thanks anyway.

RUTH. Raymond has to watch his waistline, King. His body is his instrument.

KING. (*Not knowing what to do with the extra glass, he downs it himself.*) Well, if you're sure. Cheers. Help yourself to these potato chips, folks. Now then. Down to business. As you both know, this house and the twenty-five acres behind it are all that's left of Big Jack's empire.

RUTH. Is that the Ottoman or the Holy Roman Empire?

KING. (*trying to ignore her*) What was once the seat of power and wealth for this whole county — the farm, the tannery, the sawmill, the livestock, all that has now dwindled to a falling down old ramshackledy house and twenty-five barren acres. It is sad. So sad. But I'm a dreamer. I believe in the past, and I believe in the future. Big Jack started out with nothing but this twenty-five acres and his dreams and I'm willing to do the same. I know neither one of you is interested in having anything to do with the place, and it isn't worth much, but I am willing to offer each one of you twenty-five thousand dollars for your part. (*sits on R. chair*)

RAYMOND. You've got fifty thousand dollars?

KING. I can raise it. I can raise it. My mama had a little property of her own, and my taxi cab business and my fried chicken franchise, they're flourishing. So, how about it, cousins? We got a deal?

RUTH. Aren't you forgetting something, King? The place isn't ours yet.

KING. Well, it will be in a matter of hours, Ruth. Your friend Mr. Stack's coming in the morning to read the will. Just as soon as we can get through probate, the place is ours free and clear. You and Raymond can go ahead and sell your shares to me and be on your way. We can do it tonight after supper.

RUTH. Have you seen the will?

KING. Well, naturally she'd leave it to us. What else would she do with it? We're the only living relatives. Us and your little Heather, I mean, Ray.

RUTH. Maybe she left it to Annabel Lee.

KING. Not hardly, I don't think. I know all the stories about Annabel Lee being Big Jack's bastard, and Ruth, I'll thank you not to bring that up in front of Clairice anymore.

RUTH. Well, maybe it does go to her. I mean if she was Pearl's half sister.

KING. In the first place, we don't know that for sure. Probably ain't even true. And in the second place, Pearl wouldn't be fool enough to make Annabel Lee her heir. You don't go leaving family plantations to—bastard mulattoes.

RAYMOND. By family plantation, you mean this falling down old ramshackledy house and these twenty-five barren acres?

KING. I mean to do right by Miss Anna. I've done made all the arrangements.

RUTH. What arrangements?

KING. Well, seeing as I'm the one paying for them, I don't know that I'm obliged to answer to you, but for your information, I've arranged for Miss Anna to go to the Berry Hill Nursing Home in Sparta.

RUTH. She's not sick. (*lights cigarette*)

KING. She is crazy as a bedbug. Now, Clairice and her mother drove over to Berry Hill last week, and it's a very nice place. Flower gardens and shuffleboard courts and a great big recreation room with TV's and pingpong tables. And it's integrated.

RUTH. What does Anna say about all this?

KING. Didn't seem proper to discuss it so quick after Pearl's dying.

RAYMOND. Just what is it you have in mind to do with this place, King?

KING. I have some plans which I am not at liberty to discuss right now. But that's my business. Your business is whether you want to leave here with twenty-five thousand dollars. I got all the papers ready for you to sign tonight at my house. Hey, we better be getting on down the road. What's that the poet feller says, Ruth? Miles to go before I can sleep? Clairice is really putting on the dog for you, Ray.

RUTH. Wait a minute. We're not going to your house for supper. Are we, Raymond?

RAYMOND. We're not?

RUTH. We're staying here with Anna.

KING. You know I can't bring her over to my house for supper, Ruth.

RUTH. That's fine. But Raymond and I are staying here. (*sits at piano and plays "Heart and Soul" with one finger until KING exits*)

KING. Well, I don't know about that. Raymond's free, white and twenty-one. You gon' let her boss you around like that, Ray?

RAYMOND. She always has.

KING. But Clairice is expecting you. She told all her friends. Chance Rodney's coming to her house for . . .

RAYMOND. I think Ruth's probably right.

KING. All right. All right. I tell you what. I'll go get Clairice and we'll stop by my fried chicken franchise and pick up a box of chicken and all the trimmings. We'll bring supper over here, and then we can finish up our business. Now does that suit you?

RUTH. Suit yourself.

KING. (*leaving*) Fine. Mighty glad to have you home, Ray, boy. Don't go disappearing on us before tonight now.

RAYMOND. I'm looking forward to it.

RUTH. He is such a greedy, conniving little prick.

RAYMOND. I love it when you talk dirty, baby.

RUTH. Raymond, stop it.

RAYMOND. (*wandering over to the casket*) Okay. I'll be serious. Now, here's serious. Have you looked?

RUTH. Nope.

RAYMOND. Not going to?

RUTH. (*gathering up glasses and exiting to the kitchen*) Nope.

RAYMOND. Think I'll just dive right in and have a peek. (*looks in*) Yep. That's her. More or less. (*He firmly closes lid and lies down on sofa. ANNA appears on the landing.*)

ANNA. John King? (*slowly crosses down stairs*)

RAYMOND. Miss Anna. No, it's me. Raymond.

ANNA. John King?

RAYMOND. No, mam. Raymond. Tabby's boy. Ruth's brother. I got here this afternoon. Remember?

ANNA. Raymond. Yes.

RAYMOND. I thought you said you were going to take a nap.

ANNA. Just cause I say it, don't mean I have to do it. Looks like to me your parts are getting smaller.

RAYMOND. Yes, mam. They are.

ANNA. You want to live here?

RAYMOND. Anna, we've already been through this. Yes, my parts are getting smaller, and no, I can't live here.

ANNA. I can keep house for you. You remember what a good cook I am, doncha? And the house, it'll be yours soon as I die. All yours. You like eggs goldenrod, Honey? I'm going to make some eggs goldenrod right now. Just let me go get the eggs. Gottem fresh. If there is any.

RUTH. (*offstage*) I already went. There weren't any today. Not a single egg.

ANNA. (*to RAY*) Don't tell her what we were talking about. (*aloud*) Can't stand eggs myself. Not good for anything but dogs to suck and all the dogs are dead.

RUTH. (*entering from kitchen*) I told you there aren't any eggs today.

ANNA. (*exiting to kitchen*) The hen don't like you, Ruth. She don't lay for people she don't like.

RAYMOND. They still keep chickens? (*He sits up. RUTH sits next to him.*)

RUTH. The grocery boy comes twice a week and leaves half a dozen eggs in some straw in the old hen house. Pearl paid him to. Said Anna was driving her crazy about the hen not laying. So now she lays. Six eggs twice a week.

RAYMOND. Is she always like this?

RUTH. Half the time she thinks I'm Mama.

RAYMOND. That's not unusual, is it? For someone her age?

RUTH. No, but it is unusual to think you're King Solomon's daughter.

RAYMOND. King Solomon?

RUTH. Don't you remember Sharon Rose? The biblical princess who lives inside Annabel Lee?

RAYMOND. She's still doing that?

RUTH. More than ever. Wants me to write a book about her and Sharon Rose. *The Two Faces of Anna.*

RAYMOND. Then King's right. She really is crazy.

RUTH. She gets eggs out of a hen house where there isn't even a hen. Can you do that?

RAYMOND. Ruth, you weren't serious about marrying Bobby Stack . . .

ANNA. (*enters through the kitchen carrying eggs*) Guess you just don't know which nest to look in, Ruth.

RUTH. Guess not. Here, let me help you. (*RUTH drops an egg and it cracks on the floor.*) SQ 9

ANNA. Your hands are all fluttery, Ruth. Look at that. A double yolk. It would have been twins just like you two.

RUTH. (*exiting to kitchen; sound of a car pulling up*) I'll get something to clean it up. I don't know what's the matter with me.

ANNA. We could fix this place up, you know. All it needs is some paint and a few nails.

(*KING and CLAIRICE talk as they come up the walkway.*)

CLAIRICE. I bet you anything she'll wear those blue-jeans to the funeral, and if you think I'm going . . .

KING. Here we are all ready for a picnic.

CLAIRICE. Hello again. Raymond. We were intending to entertain you in our home this evening. I was very disappointed. Needless to say.

RAYMOND. I'm sorry that didn't work out, Clairice. Ruth thought it would be better if we stayed here.

CLAIRICE. You don't have to explain to me about Ruth and what Ruth thinks. I'm used to it. I believe in making the best of a bad situation. No matter how disappointed you are. Well, we've got everything, I think. Cole slaw and okra and jalapena peppers. You prefer white meat or dark meat, Raymond?

RUTH. (*returning from kitchen with sponge and paper towels*) Anna's making eggs goldenrod for Raymond.

CLAIRICE. Oh, hey, Ruth. Who made that terrible mess?

RUTH. It's just a broken egg, Clairice.

CLAIRICE. A double yolk one. Did you break it?

RUTH. Yes. I broke it.

CLAIRICE. I bet it's bad luck. King, isn't it bad luck to break a double yolk egg?

RAYMOND. You need some help, Ruth?

RUTH. No. It's done.

CLAIRICE. I wish you could stay around for a longer time, Raymond. I'd just love to show you off. We could use another man in the family, couldn't we, Honey. It's so much responsibility for King, with all these women to take care of. And now with our baby coming and King's shopping center getting started and . . .

RAYMOND. Shopping center? I hadn't heard anything about a shopping center.

CLAIRICE. Why, darling, I thought you said they were gonna sell their parts of the property . . .

KING. That's right. That's right. I just didn't have a chance to get into the details with them about it.

RUTH. That's what you want the land for? To build a shopping center?

KING. Well, I'm not at liberty to tell you all my

business, Ruth. I have partners, and a deal like this, it has to be confidential.

CLAIRICE. I think I spoke out of turn. I just let the cat out of the bag, didn't I? Hush up, Clairice.

KING. No, no, Honey. I want my cousins to know just what kind of plans I have. You see, Ray, this isn't just any old ordinary shopping center I'm gonna build here. No sir. It's going to be a monument to our family. And I am dedicating it especially to the finest Christian lady who ever lived. Our grandmother, Beulah Samuels Vaughnum.

RAYMOND. Do they dedicate shopping centers to women down here now?

KING. I told you, this isn't just any kind of shopping center. Not just anybody can rent space in it. Only Christians.

RUTH. Any color Christians?

KING. No liquor stores, no dirty books. A place for Christian merchants to dwell and sell in the name of the Lord.

RAYMOND. What do you plan to call this temple of free enterprise, King?

KING. That's the best part. I bet you could guess it if you tried.

RUTH. What?

ANNA. (*entering with a dish which she gives RAY-MOND*) Here you are, Honey. Eggs goldenrod.

KING. Come on. Guess. You ready? Beulah Land.

CLAIRICE. Isn't that just wonderful? Beulah Land. After Miss Beulah and for the hymn.

ANNA. (*starts singing the hymn "Beulahland" and continues through the following dialogue*) . . . I'm dwelling in the . . . (*continues*)

RUTH. Oh Jesus.

CLAIRICE. King, Miss Anna's making me nervous.

KING. That's enough now, Miss Anna. I say that's enough. (*ANNA continues singing.*) I guess you can see what I mean about Miss Anna now, Ray. Miss Anna, be quiet now please.

RUTH. What did you have in mind to give Anna, King?

KING. Give her? I told you I plan to pay all her bills at the Berry Hill Nursing Home. Ain't that enough? (*ANNA stops singing abruptly and stares at KING.*) Well, now, Miss Anna, I had intended to wait until after the funeral to discuss this with you, but I guess now's as good a time as any. Naturally, with Aunt Pearl passed on, you wouldn't be able to stay here. So Clairice and her mother found this real nice place in Sparta where there's plenty of nice people to take care of you and . . .

ANNA. (*speaking now as SHARON ROSE*) I come to my garden, my sister my bride. I gather my myrrh with my spice.

KING. Now don't start that. We're trying to have a serious conversation here.

ANNA. I eat my honeycomb with my honey. I drink my wine with my milk. A garden fountain, a well of living water and flowing streams from Lebanon. Oh that thou were as my brother that sucked the breasts of my mother. When I should find thee without, I would kiss thee. I would lead thee and bring thee into my mother's

KING. Goddam it, Miss Anna. Now listen. It's late. It's time for Sharon Rose to go to bed. Time to go night night, Princess Sharon Rose. You go on to sleep now. I need to talk to Annabel Lee. Sweet dreams, Princess Sharon Rose. (*ANNA stops.*)

house. Solomon had a
vineyard at . . .

KING. Now. I know this is kind of sudden, and I understand you're still in a state of shock about Aunt Pearl. But I assure you—

ANNA. (*as herself*) No.

KING. Well, just what do you propose to do, may I ask?

ANNA. Nothing.

KING. You can't do nothing. You have to do something.

CLAIRICE. Miss Anna, maybe if we drove over to Berry Hill . . .

KING. That's a good idea. We could drive over tomorrow right after the . . .

ANNA. This is my house, and I'm staying here.

KING. Well, I'm afraid that's just the point. This is not your house. Now that Aunt Pearl's gone, it belongs to Ruth and Raymond and me. And if you'd been paying attention awhile ago, you'd a heard me telling about my plans to build the Beulah Land Shopping Mall on this property. Now I'm mighty sorry if that don't suit you, but under the circumstances, I think I'm being very generous.

ANNA. Big Jack left it to me.

KING. Big Jack! We're not concerned with Big Jack now, goddamit. It's Aunt Pearl's will we're talking about.

CLAIRICE. King Vaughnum!

ANNA. Pearl's got nothing to do with it.

KING. Well, I beg to differ.

CLAIRICE. King Vaughnum, do you realize the words that just came out of your mouth?

ANNA. Wasn't up to Pearl to say who got the property. Big Jack left it in a life estate.

CLAIRICE. King, did you hear me?

KING. What the hell does that mean, a life estate?

ANNA. Means my life and my estate.

KING. I never saw any will like that.

RUTH. Anna's seen it.

KING. The devil she has.

CLAIRICE. Y'all, we better go on and eat. This chicken's getting cold.

KING. Let me see that will.

RUTH. Oh, you'll see it soon enough. Here, Clairice, let me help you.

CLAIRICE. Wait, now. We have to say the blessing. King? Daddy, will you say grace?

KING. Well, if she's seen it, I oughta be able to see it.

CLAIRICE. King!

KING. What?

CLAIRICE. Would you please say grace for us?

KING. Lord, we thank thee for what we are about to partake of. Bless this house and thy servants in it. Amen. Ruth, I do not appreciate this.

CLAIRICE. Okay, everybody. Dig in.

KING. Shit. (*crosses* U.R., *CLAIRICE follows*)

CLAIRICE. I am very disappointed in your language, and I for one am not speaking to you until you apologize. Raymond, do you prefer (*crosses to RAY-MOND*) white or dark meat? I know I asked you that before, but in all this yelling, I forgot what you said.

RAYMOND. That's fine, Clairice. A thigh will be fine.

CLAIRICE. Ruth, would you ask King what piece he prefers.

RUTH. Certainly. King, would you care for a drumstick or a thigh or a . . .

KING. Clairice, I don't think you understand the full

significance of what is happening here.

CLAIRICE. I'm sure if you will just calm down and stop taking the Lord's name in vain, Miss Anna will change her mind. Now, Miss Anna, what piece would you prefer?

ANNA. A neck or a gizzard. (*KING, realizing what CLAIRICE means, quickly changes his approach.*)

KING. Ha ha. Fraid we don't cook necks and gizzards. Most people don't care for 'em. Not everybody appreciates those parts like you and me, Miss Anna. How about a nice juicy breast? You want some cole slaw? Clairice, get Miss Anna some cole slaw. Well, now. Seeing as how you may be a woman of property now, ha ha, I guess you and me needs to talk a little business. I'm prepared to make you a good offer for the land, Miss Anna. And if you don't feel like you'd be happy living at Berry Hill, well then you could buy you another house with the money from this sale. This old house is mighty drafty in the winters.

ANNA. Sure is.

KING. Yes, it is. Matter of fact, there's a little house over on Pike Street for sale right now. We go right by there every day, don't we, Clairice. Why we'd be able to drop by and look in on you once in awhile. I bet we could get you moved in inside a week. And Clairice and I would like to give you a little housewarming present. Something I bet you'd really enjoy.

CLAIRICE. What?

KING. A color TV. Wouldn't you like that, Miss Anna? A color TV? Like I said before, you're just like one of us, and we feel responsible for taking care of you. Matter of fact, Miss Anna, you probably don't know it, but lots of folks around here used to say you *was* part of the family.

CLAIRICE. King!

KING. Well, we're all grown up people, Clairice. And if Miss Anna's our natural kin, she has a right to know about it.

RUTH. King, this is disgusting.

KING. What I am referring to, Miss Anna, is that folks used to say that you were Big Jack's illegitimate daughter.

CLAIRICE. King, just ask yourself. What would the church say about this?

KING. We're not talking right or wrong here, Clairice. We're talking reality. (*CLAIRICE begins to make several trips to the kitchen clearing dishes and food, showing obvious annoyance with KING. RUTH helps.*) And the men in this family have a responsibility to atone for the sins of our fathers. You feel the same way, don't you, Raymond?

RAYMOND. About the sins of our fathers? You bet.

KING. Course, we don't have any way of knowing for sure. Less Miss Anna knows and has been keeping it a secret. But we all know what a vital and lusty man Big Jack was. Right, Ray?

RAYMOND. A real man for all seasons.

KING. So we just have to accept the truth and stop trying to hide our skeletons under the bed. Miss Anna's a legitimate member of this family. She is one of us.

RUTH. I'd give it a lot of thought, Anna, before I decided to become one of us.

KING. This don't concern you, Ruth. What would you say to twenty-thousand dollars, Miss Anna?

ANNA. (*getting up*) My place is not for sale.

KING. Well, now wait a minute. I'm willing to negotiate. Where you going?

ANNA. I got to get up early to get Pearl ready for the funeral.

KING. Now wait a minute, I said. I'm making you a

good offer. The place'll come to us when you die, anyway. You ain't got nobody else to leave it to. I'm offering to make you a rich woman. Thirty thousand dollars.

ANNA. (*starting upstairs, speaking as SHARON ROSE*) Solomon had a vineyard in Baalhamon. He let out the vineyard

ANNA. (*continued*) to keepers. My vineyard is for myself.

I am the Rose of Sharon.

The lily of the valley.
I am black but comely.
Oh ye daughters of Jerusalem.

CLAIRICE. (*returns from kitchen, picks up box containing chicken from downstage table. She experiences a sudden pain, grasps her stomach and drops box, spilling chicken on floor. She is helped to sofa by RUTH and RAYMOND.*) Ohhh. Something's happening.

KING. (*following ANNA to the landing, oblivious of CLAIRICE's situation*) Don't start with that again, godammit. I'm trying to talk business to you. Forty thousand.

RAYMOND. King, something's wrong.

RUTH. King, for God's sakes.

KING. Annabel Lee, you come back down here. Fifty thousand!

BLACKOUT

End of Act One

ACT TWO

As the lights come up, RUTH and RAYMOND are sit- SQ 10
ting on the glider on the porch, singing favorites
from their youth. It is late evening. They laugh and
horse around and are generally having a good time,
feeling comfortable and at home for the first time.
If possible, RAYMOND plays on an old guitar.
They sing a portion of a classic rock'n'roll song of
the late 50's.

RAYMOND. Oh, Elvis, Elvis, Elvis. Where have all the
young girls gone?

RUTH. How many do you need?

RAYMOND. Ah, Ruthie. What happened to the hopes
we had then?

RUTH. You mean when you were going to be the next
James Dean, and I was the next Sylvia Plath? We
haven't exactly fulfilled our youthful promise, have we?
I've published three slim volumes of poetry, each one
slimmer than the one before, and to quote Annabel Lee,
teach poem writing to a lot of pimply faced rednecks.
And you . . .

RAYMOND. Oh please. I don't think I want to hear
this.

RUTH. You, Chance Rodney, world class heart-
breaker, are now in your fifth year on "All Our Yesterdays" . . .

RAYMOND. Where my parts are getting smaller.

RUTH. Will you lose the soap?

RAYMOND. Oh sure. Just a matter of time. I expect
old Chance will be dead before Christmas.

RUTH. What will you do?

RAYMOND. I don't know. Maybe retire. Take a trip

around the world. Five years on a soap can be very lucrative. I'm thinking about writing a book about it.

RUTH. About the life on a soap opera? Who'd read it?

RAYMOND. Clairice. You laugh. There are a lot of Clairice's out there. Just dying to go behind the scenes with Chance Rodney. I wanted to be a great actor. I tried. Wasn't great. But I was pretty good. Good enough to become rich and famous making love in the afternoon. (*They both laugh.*)

RUTH. You won't miss it? "All Our Yesterdays."

RAYMOND. If I do, I'll find something else. It's just a job, Ruth. It's not life. It's certainly not art.

RUTH. What is?

RAYMOND. Art?

RUTH. No. Life.

RAYMOND. I think it's this.

RUTH. Honeysuckle Hill?

RAYMOND. Ah huh. The pecan tree, the hen house with its imaginary hen, the pond down behind the cemetery.

RUTH. The whole place is a cemetery, if you ask me.

RAYMOND. I don't want it to be a shopping center. (*pause*) Are you going to marry Bobby Stack?

RUTH. Where did that come from?

RAYMOND. I just want to know. Are you seriously considering marrying him?

RUTH. No. Not right now. But he's a nice person, and he's not stupid. In a few years, if he's still asking, I might. I'd kind of like to have someone to grow old with. Wouldn't you?

RAYMOND. There are worse things than being alone. Being married to the wrong person, for example.

RUTH. What about the girl now?

RAYMOND. A distraction. A very pretty, fresh-faced

one, but not especially different from the one before her
or the one who'll come after. They usually last about six
weeks. Then they start crying. That's when I know it's
time to move on.

RUTH. And you just drop that one and go on to the
next?

RAYMOND. Well, there's usually some time in between.

KING. (*coming up the walk, a man with a purpose*)
All right. Where's Miss Anna.

RUTH. She's gone to bed.

KING. Well get her up. I gotta talk business with her.

RAYMOND. Is Clairice all right?

KING. She's fine. Ruth, I need to talk to Miss Anna.

RUTH. I told you. She's already gone to bed. You can
talk to her tomorrow.

RAYMOND. Is she still at the hospital?

KING. Doc Brady wanted to keep her there overnight
just to keep an eye on her. But he says she's fine. Baby's
fine. Just a false alarm. I need to talk to her now.

RAYMOND. Well that's good news. She gave us all a
scare.

KING. I'll say. Scared me nearly to death. Ruth, would
you just go see if Miss Anna's still awake?

RUTH. No, I won't. She's tired and she's old, and I'm
not going . . .

RAYMOND. You could just look in on her, couldn't
you, Ruth. If she's asleep, I'm sure King wouldn't want
to disturb her. Would you, King?

KING. No. Of course not. But if she's just sitting up
there wide awake . . .

RAYMOND. That's fair, Ruthie.

RUTH. (*Starting in the house, they follow.*) All right.
I'll go up and see. If she's awake, I'll call you. But I

know she's not, and I'm not waking her up.

KING. Lots of time old people can't sleep, you know. They're up all hours of the night. Just staring at the walls.

RAYMOND. How about a nightcap, King? (*RAYMOND exits to kitchen.*)

KING. That's a mighty good idea. I could sure use one. This has been some kind of day. I tell you. First this business 'bout the will and Miss Anna. Then Clairice. Doc Brady, he put these little wires on Clairice's stomach, and you could watch these little blips on a machine up on the wall. Blip, blip, blip. I said, "Doc, what's that mean?" (*RAYMOND enters with 2 glasses and vodka bottle.*) And he said, "Means he's still in there kicking." Ha ha. Little feller's still in there kicking. Made me so happy, I couldn't hardly take my eyes off a that machine. Just blippin away. I guess you know how I feel. You know how it feels, being a father.

RAYMOND. Yeah.

KING. Ain't no other feeling like it.

RAYMOND. Nope. It's one of a kind, that feeling. Here you go.

KING. Thank you, well, here's to us daddies.

RAYMOND. To fatherhood.

KING. You know, if you ask me, that's one thing this family hasn't been too good at. Fathers, I mean. Mothers too, for that matter.

RAYMOND. No. We have not excelled in the area of fathers and mothers.

KING. I didn't mean you, you understand. I'm sure you're a fine father to little Heather, even being divorced and all. But our mamas and daddies, they just wasn't able to give us much of a normal kind of family life. Not that it was their fault. Being sick and dying and all. My mama just kind a gave up living after Daddy and Aunt Tabby died. And your daddy getting killed in the war. I'm sure he was a good man. Course he was gone before I was even born.

RAYMOND. He was gone before we saw much of him either.

KING. Big Jack was always bragging about his son-in-law, the hero of the Normandy landing.

RAYMOND. It was a war for heroes.

KING. They gave your mama a medal and flag. I know that. She was a sweet lady, Aunt Tabiatha. Real pretty too.

RAYMOND. They were all sweet people. My mama and daddy, your mama and daddy. Sweet people. They just lacked . . . staying power.

KING. Well, they're all in heaven now.

RAYMOND. Let's hope so.

KING. I know so. You know, I's just eight years old the day Daddy got killed on the tractor and your mama . . . died. But I remember it like it was yesterday. Aunt Pearl telephoned up to our house and said Tabiatha had done took a bunch of sleeping pills and killed herself. Mama sent old Nathan out in the field to find Daddy, and she brought me up here to this house. We were sitting on this sofa right here when Nathan came in and said he found Mr. John King lying out in the field with the tractor rolled over on him. Mama wouldn't believe it. Just too much all at once to get a hold of. Lots of folks say Aunt Tabby killed herself out of grief cause her twin was dead, but course that isn't true.

RAYMOND. You don't think so?

KING. No. She couldn't a known Daddy was dead. No way she could of. Nobody did. Just one of those crazy coincidences like you read about.

RAYMOND. Maybe.

KING. No maybe about it. You don't believe in all that ESP stuff?

RAYMOND. I don't know.

KING. Well, I can tell you. It was a coincidence. A coincidence to us, I mean. In the mind of God it was all planned out, of course. I guess He planned it that way because they were twins. God figured those two came into the world together and they oughta go out of it together.

RAYMOND. That's pretty elementary logic for the mind of God, isn't it?

KING. Mysterious ways. Ours not to reason why. All we can do is just live the best possible life we can while we're here on earth and let the lord take us when he will. One thing I can tell you, though. What we were talking about before. I plan to have the right kind of family life for me and Clairice and our baby. A real normal kind of family. With good dinners every night and basketball games and toys and all that. And noise. Lots of noise. TV sets with the Sugar Bowl playing and screen doors slamming and like that. That's what I want more than anything. A normal life. That's the most important thing.

RAYMOND. Well, good luck to you, sir. Let's drink to a normal life.

KING. I'll sure drink to that. Whoops. Have to have another drink to drink to that with. (*KING pours himself another drink and freshens RAYMOND's drink.*) I'm not really a drinking man anymore, but this is a special occasion, isn't it? No telling when I'll have another opportunity to talk about old times with my favorite cousin. You're leaving tomorrow, I guess.

RAYMOND. Ummm. Tomorrow night. We don't actually have much in the way of old times to talk about, do we, King? I mean you were just a little boy when I left.

KING. I know it's not like we grew up together. But like I said this afternoon, we share the same heritage. You and me. And Ruth. Although Ruth don't seem to have much use for her heritage. Funny thing. Her being a poet and all. (*up*) I always thought writers was the ones that cared the most about what they come from. Like William Faulkner and Jack London. That's what they're supposed to write about, isn't it?

RAYMOND. I imagine Ruth's writing about what she comes from. In her way.

KING. Mighty funny way. (*KING picks up a thin volume from bookcase.*) These poems of hers, they're not about the South. I can tell you that. Less you call below the waist the South. Doing it. That's what Ruth writes about.

RAYMOND. Doing it?

KING. Yeah. Sex. That's what our Ruth's got on her little mind. Every one of these things is about doing it or pretending to do it, or what women think up in their heads while they're doing it. I told Clairice not to read 'em.

RAYMOND. But you did.

KING. Well, she is my cousin. You read 'em?

RAYMOND. Some.

KING. Well, you tell me then. What's she talking about besides sex?

RAYMOND. (*taking the book from KING*) Oh, loneliness, memory, broken dreams.

KING. Well! You're a better man than I am, Gunga Din.

RAYMOND. I see you know something about poetry yourself.

KING. Little bit. I took a course when I was at Junior College. The course was really about writing themes, but we studied some poems. Rudyard Kipling, he's the one wrote Gunga Din, he's my favorite. You can understand what he's saying, and he talks about life and important things like that. "If you can hold your head up when all about you are losing theirs and blaming it on you. If you can trust yourself when all men doubt you and make allowance for their doubting too; If you can dream and not make dreams your master. If you can think . . . (*During poem RAYMOND returns book to bookcase, picks up bottle and glasses.*)

RAYMOND. Eh, too bad about your shopping center, King.

KING. What's that?

RAYMOND. Your shopping center. The Beulah Land Shopping Mall where Christian merchants dwell and sell in the name of the Lord? I like that. You going to look for another piece of land now or just forget about it?

KING. Ha ha. Not likely. Neither one. I'm going right ahead. In a year's time, the Beulah Land Shopping Mall will be right where you're standing.

RAYMOND. But if the property belongs to Annabel Lee, and she won't sell . . .

KING. Ho ho. I don't give up a dream that easy. In the first place, that will Miss Anna's seen may not even be the right one. And if it is, then I'll just have to get her to listen to reason. I can be pretty persuasive, you know.

RAYMOND. What if you're not persuasive enough? She can be pretty stubborn.

KING. Then I'll just have to get a judge to understand that Miss Anna ain't able to take care of her own affairs and put me in charge. Anybody can see she's half crazy. Couldn't stay here by herself anyway.

RAYMOND. She could if someone lived with her.

(*RAYMOND exits to kitchen with bottle and glasses.*)

KING. Who's gon' do that? I sure ain't. Clairice'd have a duck fit if I suggested we come live here with that old . . . You're not thinking about it, are you? Naw, course you're not. Be kinda hard to make a living in the soap opera business down here, wouldn't it?

RAYMOND. (*enters*) Yeah, it would. But Ruth might.

KING. Ruth. Ha ha. Not likely. Miss Ruth ain't thinking about living here. I can tell you that. Got no appreciation of the past, Ruth don't. Besides, she likes her privacy, if you know what I mean. She don't even have a telephone. I'm a good judge of character, and I can tell you, that girl ain't gon' come here and take care of some crazy old woman. No, sir. Not our Ruth.

RUTH. (*coming downstairs*) Not our Ruth what?

KING. Oh, hey there, Ruth. Nothin, Honey. Nothin at all. What about Miss Anna?

RUTH. What about her?

KING. She coming down?

RUTH. Oh. No. She's sound asleep.

KING. Oh.

RAYMOND. (*moving KING toward the door*) It's pretty late, King. Why don't I run you home on the motorcycle.

KING. Oh I'm not walking. Got one of my taxi cabs waiting. You tell Miss Anna I'll come over in the morning to talk to her.

RAYMOND. (*walking KING out on the porch*) I'll tell her. We'll see you tomorrow then, King. You get some rest.

KING. (*down the walk*) I will. I will. Sure can use it. Night night, Ruth. (*sound of a car pulling away*)   SQ 11

RAYMOND. (*coming back in the living room where*

RUTH is looking at things in the trunk) King's not really such a bad sort, is he?

RUTH. (*absorbed in the trunk*) He's a prince.

RAYMOND. Really. He may not be sensitive and urbane like us, but in his way, he's all right. He just wants to be happy.

RUTH. What's special about him that he should be happy?

RAYMOND. It wouldn't hurt you to have a little tolerance, Ruth.

RUTH. And it wouldn't hurt you to have a little discernment.

RAYMOND. All I said was that King wasn't so bad. What's wrong with that?

RUTH. It's a sucker's attitude. That's what's wrong with it. Don't be fooled by the way King was just now. He's one of those people who's less obnoxious when he's scared or drunk. He's family, and we're stuck with him, but that doesn't mean we have to be taken in by him.

RAYMOND. He means to get this place one way or another. (*pause*) You gonna let him have it?

RUTH. This is Anna's fight, not mine. (*continues to pull items out of trunk*)

RAYMOND. That's courageous. What's all that stuff?

RUTH. Mama's things. Anna brought it in. See. Mama's fox. You remember that picture of Mama and Daddy and us when we were babies? Daddy has on his uniform, and Mama has on her fur. And this suit. We missed all the style.

RAYMOND. I think you've got plenty of style.

RUTH. What were you and King talking about when I came downstairs?

RAYMOND. Your coming here and living with Anna.

RUTH. That'll be the day.

RAYMOND. That's what King said. Said he was a good judge of character, and that girl ain't gon' come here and take care of some crazy old woman.

RUTH. He's right.

RAYMOND. No, sir. Not our Ruth.

RUTH. No, sir. Not our Ruth.

RAYMOND. Are you sure? I mean, have you really thought about it? It would be good for you to have the place someday, and Sparta's only twenty minutes away. Less, the way you drive. You know Anna won't be able to stay here if you don't. King's already . . .

RUTH. Not my problem. And I'll tell you the same thing I told her. I don't want this damn place. Now or ever. If we get some money out of it, fine. If not, that's fine too. But I'm not coming here to live. This is my last night at Honeysuckle Hill.

RAYMOND. Have you actually read the will?

RUTH. What do I know about reading wills? It's in there. (*Pointing to trunk; RUTH exits kitchen.*)

RAYMOND. (*starting to rummage through the trunk*) Well, let's have a look. You could sell it when Anna dies.

RUTH. (*enters, turns off fan and some interior lights*) Uh huh. And I could write a book about her and Sharon Rose. If you're so hot to have Anna keep the place, you do it. You come here and live with her.

RAYMOND. Me?

RUTH. Sure, why not. You've got plenty of money. You could return it to the way it was at the height of Big Jack's manhood. (*RAYMOND is absorbed in the will and ignores her.*) What's it say. (*pause*) It does go to Anna, doesn't it?

RAYMOND. It says the property is left in a life estate to

the natural children of Jack Vaughnum. At the death of his last natural child, the place goes to the surviving grandchildren and they can sell it if none of them wants to live on it. Anna thinks since she's a natural child, it's hers.

RUTH. Well, if she is his natural child . . .

RAYMOND. She can't prove that, Ruth. It doesn't name her by name. King won't waste five minutes challenging that in court.

RUTH. Will he win?

RAYMOND. I don't know. I'm not a lawyer. Ask your friend Bobby. But my guess is she wouldn't stand a chance.

RUTH. What if we both testified that she was his daughter?

RAYMOND. All we could say is that we think she was. We don't have any proof. Anna doesn't even know for sure.

RUTH. Maybe there is proof. Maybe there's a birth certificate or a note or something. (*crosses to trunk*)

RAYMOND. Get serious. There isn't going to be a birth certificate for an illegitimate black child born seventy-five years ago. And if there were, it would hardly identify the father as Big Jack Vaughnum.

RUTH. You have a better idea? It's our only chance. Anna's only chance.

RAYMOND. An infinitesimal one.

RUTH. We can at least try. We have to at least do that for her.

RAYMOND. I thought this wasn't your problem. All right. I'll run over to Sparta in the morning and look through the records in the courthouse. But I can tell you now, it's a wild goose chase. Looks like it's up to you,

Ruth. You want Anna to have this place, you'll have to have it with her.

RUTH. That's so like you, Raymond. You think it would be fine for me to come bury myself here, but not you. Not lively enough for Chance Rodney. Not enough Lolitas to keep him entertained.

RAYMOND. Now wait a minute. Just because you feel guilty, don't try to make me the heavy here.

RUTH. Guilty? Why should I feel guilty?

RAYMOND. Don't ask me. You're the one who says she doesn't care what happens to the place, and then wants to chase all over the county looking for some damn birth certificate. Don't blame me because you're here, and I'm not. You could have stayed away. Why didn't you?

RUTH. I came home to see if I'd kill myself like Mama did.

RAYMOND. Well, did you?

RUTH. I mean, if I was going to do it, this is certainly the place, right?

RAYMOND. The world is too cruel for most people, Ruth. But they don't put on a pink peignoir and climb into bed and swallow a bottle of sleeping pills because their brother's dead.

RUTH. Then I passed the age Mama was when she died, and surprise, I hadn't done it. By then I was too old to take off again.

RAYMOND. You're not old.

RUTH. We're not young either. Our lives are half over, brother. By the time Mama and Uncle John King were our age, they'd married and had their children and were dead. So we're on the home stretch, aren't we? The home stretch to what?

RAYMOND. You didn't have to come back here for

that. Mortality's not a singularly Southern predicament, you know. It's a universal condition, Honey. We all feel life slipping through our fingers day by day and want it to mean more than it does. (*puts articles in trunk, closes lid, sits on trunk*)

RUTH. Do you ever think about coming home? For good?

RAYMOND. No.

RUTH. You said yourself you won't be on "All Our Yesterdays" much longer. If you lived here, Heather could come at Christmas (*sits on trunk*) and in the summers. She'd love it here.

RAYMOND. No.

RUTH. Don't you think she'd love it? She'd be in heaven going through all the old stuff in the smokehouse and the pantry like we used to when we were . . .

RAYMOND. We're not talking about Heather. (*pause*) You know why I can't come back here.

RUTH. Why?

RAYMOND. For the same reason I left twenty years ago and haven't been back for more than three days at a time since.

RUTH. Why?

RAYMOND. You know why, goddammit. Why are you doing this? (*up, crosses* L.)

RUTH. Because I want to hear you say it. Twenty years is a long time.

RAYMOND. All right, sister. You got it. We have had a rather unnatural attraction for each other ever since Mama stopped bathing us in the same bathtub. And if I lived here and you lived fifteen miles away, it is quite possible that the not very fraternal flirtation we indulge in would . . . and that we, dear sister, would . . .

RUTH. Still can't say it, can you?

RAYMOND. This isn't a joking matter.

RUTH. What else is it but a joke? I mean, why not? Neither one of us has ever had a decent relationship with anyone else. And we've both pretty well covered the waterfront.

RAYMOND. I can't believe you're saying this.

RUTH. You said it first. (*up*)

RAYMOND. You baited me into it. And I just suggested the existence of the idea. I didn't suggest . . .

RUTH. Then you don't want to.

RAYMOND. I didn't say that. I just didn't expect to . . . For one thing, it's probably against the law. You mean you'd actually . . . do that? You'd . . . what's wrong?

RUTH. My cheeks are burning. Not as brave as I thought I was.

RAYMOND. We've been leading up to it forever, haven't we. Ruth . . . my whole life has been what I did because I couldn't have you.

RUTH. Do you want us to be lovers? Just once?

RAYMOND. It's not a question of what I want. It's . . .

RUTH. A question of discernment? And courage?

RAYMOND. Yes, dammit. And a lot of other things.

RUTH. I don't think so. (*pause*) You know what you said before about if I lived in Sparta and you lived here? You know what that made me think of?

RAYMOND. What?

RUTH. That game Mama and Daddy used to play with us when they put us to bed. (*RUTH traces the pattern of the child's game on his face, forehead, chin, circle around the cheek, then quickly down from forehead across nose to chin. Their eyes do not move from each other's until the blackout.*) If you lived up here, and I lived down here, would you go way around here to see me? Or would you just jump the ditch?

(*As her finger crosses his face, RAYMOND grabs her* SQ 12
   wrist and holds it.
Blackout. SQ 13
*The next morning. As the lights come up ANNA is iron-
   ing a dress. She hums "Go Tell Aunt Rhody the Old
   Gray Goose is Dead." RUTH comes down the
   stairs, her hair still tangled from sleeping.*)

RUTH. Where's Raymond?

ANNA. Took off early this morning. Went over to
Sparta.

RUTH. Oh. (*RUTH looks out the window.*)

ANNA. Something the matter with you?

RUTH. What would be the matter with me?

ANNA. I'm asking you. You look like something the
cat drug in.

RUTH. Thanks. What are you ironing?

ANNA. Dress to put on Pearl to bury her in.

RUTH. Why?

ANNA. You can't bury somebody in their nightgown.

RUTH. They would have done all that at the funeral
home if you'd let them.

ANNA. Pearl wouldn't a liked men messing with her
body. Even dead.

RUTH. The grave's a fine and private place, but none I
think do there embrace. (*pause*) Did you ever sleep with
a man?

ANNA. None of your business. Less you want to write
a book about me.

RUTH. Never mind.

ANNA. Reckon he'll be leaving after the funeral.

RUTH. Tonight, I think. Is there any coffee?

ANNA. It's on the stove. (*RUTH goes into the kitchen
leaving the door open. They continue to converse.*)

RUTH. You know Bobby's coming this morning.

ANNA. Don't matter to me. I know what the will says.

RUTH. Looks like it's going to rain.

ANNA. That's Raymond's a sweet boy. Always was. (*RUTH returns with her coffee, thunder is heard.*) You   SQ 14 shouldn't let him go off again.

RUTH. I'm not his mother.

ANNA. I done told him I thought he oughta stay here.

RUTH. What'd he say?

ANNA. Said no. But he might listen to you.

RUTH. He doesn't belong here.

ANNA. Belongs where you are. That's where he belongs.

RUTH. What are you talking about?

ANNA. You and Raymond. You don't have nobody else. Either one of you. Y'all know something about each other don't nobody else know.

RUTH. What?

ANNA. I don't know. Nobody does but y'all. Tabby and John King was like that too. Cause you're twins, I reckon. Like one's the key and one's the lock.

RUTH. Well, I guess I'll just have to stay locked up.

ANNA. Huh. Maybe you're the key.

RUTH. And maybe you're the Rose of Sharon. Anna? You know King may win. You may not be able to stay here.

ANNA. Maybe.

RUTH. What'll you do?

ANNA. You want this ring off of Pearl's finger?

RUTH. Why would I want it?

ANNA. It was Miss Beulah's wedding ring.

RUTH. I don't wear rings. Why don't you keep it?

ANNA. Got no claim to it.

RUTH. Give it to Clairice then. She'd love it.

ANNA. Reckon I'll just leave it on Pearl. (*holding the*

dress up in front of her) That's good enough. Won't be long before it rots anyway.

RUTH. Why are you doing this? Ironing that dress, fixing her up. You don't have to.

ANNA. Yes, I do.

RUTH. But you didn't love her. She was hateful to you.

ANNA. Not all the time, she wasn't. I don't know if I loved her or not. Maybe I hated her. In the end it don't matter much. They're all feelings. Love ain't the only tie that binds, Ruth. (*pause*) Will you come live here with me?

RUTH. No. Anna, if I could help you, I would. But there's too much sadness here, too many . . . There's no life here for me. (*RUTH gets suit out of trunk.*)

ANNA. (*looks at RUTH for a moment, then moves toward the casket*) Well, I gotta get Pearl ready. That funeral wagon'll be driving up pretty soon. (*ANNA opens the casket, puts the ring back on Pearl's finger.*) Pretty little Pearl.

RUTH. (*trying to change the mood*) We have any eggs?

ANNA. Nope.

RUTH. Old hen's not laying again, huh? (*RUTH starts ironing suit.*)

ANNA. Can't.

RUTH. Why not?

ANNA. Cause there ain't no hen.

RUTH. What?

ANNA. Now you ain't gonna stand there and tell me you think there's live chickens out there in that hen house.

RUTH. But I thought you thought . . .

ANNA. I did. Couple of times it just slipped my mind

we didn't have chickens anymore, and I went out to fetch the eggs. Pearl got it in her head I'se crazy, and she started having 'em deliver the eggs out there so I could find 'em. I wasn't crazy. Least not all the time. I just forgot. Anybody can forget. But once Pearl made up her mind to pacify me, I had to keep on fetching those damn eggs to pacify her. She loved to do things that made her feel better'n other people. Like she's rich and other people's poor, or she's smart and other people's dumb. Or crazy.

RUTH. (*laughing*) You mean you've been letting her . . .

ANNA. That's right. If I'd a told her I knew there wasn't any hen out there and to stop making that boy put those eggs in the straw . . . Shoot. She'd a sulked for a month. Maybe now she's gone we could get some real hens and have some real eggs to fetch.

RUTH. Wouldn't it be easier to just let the boy deliver them to the kitchen?

ANNA. Chickens are a lot of company. You get eggs from them. And they make a nice friendly kind of noise. You can eat 'em. Ain't a lot of trouble. Not like them good for nothing dogs your grandaddy kept round the place.

RUTH. Those were hunting dogs.

ANNA. Huh. How many times you recollect seeing him go hunting with them?

RUTH. I don't know. He was always talking about it.

ANNA. Only time I ever remember him taking those dogs hunting was one time when I'se a little bitty girl. Him and Nathan was gone two days, and when they come back, they had a doe. Shot through the neck. Miss Beulah ran out in the yard and saw that doe hanging dead with its feet tied up on a stick. Lord, she started crying and hitting on your grandaddy. He kept trying to tell her it was an accident. Didn't mean to shoot a doe.

Said he thought it was a buck. Wasn't nothing he could say would ease Miss Beulah. Kept crying 'bout some little baby deer out there in the woods looking for its mama, and it wasn't gon' find her, cause he'd murdered her. Only way Big Jack could get any peace was to cart that doe off and promise he wouldn't go hunting anymore. Even then she wouldn't hardly speak to him for the longest time. Humph. If you ask me, it was 'cause a that dead doe that Tabiatha and John King wasn't born for another ten years after that.

RUTH. (*amused*) You think she refused to sleep with him for ten years because he killed a doe? (*folds ironing board and takes iron and board off-stage, returning immediately*)

ANNA. I'se too little to think that then, but looking back on it, wouldn't surprise me. Miss Beulah wasn't as sweet and timid as everybody thought. You reckon you could help me get this dress on Pearl?

RUTH. Eh, I don't think I could . . .

ANNA. You don't have to touch her. Just hold the dress so I can get her arms through the sleeves.   SQ 15

RUTH. I'd better go get dressed myself. They'll be here, and I'll still be standing here looking like something the cat drug in. I think I hear a car now. Why don't you just lay the dress on top of her? I mean, nobody's going to see her from behind. (*RUTH runs up the stairs. ANNA looks after her a second, then returns to trying to get the dress on Pearl.*)

ANNA. Hold still, now.

(*Noise on the walk, as KING and CLAIRICE enter. CLAIRICE is in a wheelchair, and KING pushes.*)

CLAIRICE. I feel just ridiculous in this thing. Like I was an invalid or something.

KING. I'm not taking any chances with you, Mrs.
Vaughnum. Until that baby's born, you're not going to
so much as pick up a spoon.   SQ 15A

CLAIRICE. Wait a minute. I'm caught on the screen.
King, you're gonna tear a hole in my dress. There. All
right. Forward march. (*ANNA stares at them as they
come through the door.*)

KING. Morning, Miss Anna. Looks like we may not
have the best weather for the funeral.

ANNA. She gone lame on you?

CLAIRICE. See there. She's making fun of me. I knew
she would.

KING. Clairice is in a very delicate condition here.

ANNA. Well, wheel her over there. She's blocking out
my light. Getting real dark out there. (*ANNA starts to
lift the top part of Pearl's body up high enough to be
visible.*)

CLAIRICE. Aiiii—

KING. What the hell do you think you're doing?

ANNA. I'm trying to get Pearl dressed for her own
funeral. And I could use some help.

CLAIRICE. Oh, I can't believe this.

KING. You cannot be changing the clothes on a dead
body right here in the living room for all to see. Now
close that casket.

ANNA. I shoulda picked a dress that didn't button
down the back.

KING. All right. Here. I'll stand in front. Clairice,
close your eyes just to be on the safe side.

ANNA. I could use some help.

KING. Just get it done and close that lid. (*KING
stands with his back to the casket, facing CLAIRICE
and the audience. He spreads his arms wide to conceal
the casket as much as possible. CLAIRICE squeezes her*

*eyes shut. KING closes his eyes too. ANNA fumbles
with the body for a minute, then lets it drop flat.*)

ANNA. There. (*ANNA closes the casket. CLAIRICE
opens her eyes. KING drops his arms and turns around.
ANNA stands there with a long white nightgown
thrown over her shoulder.*)

KING. Now then. Why don't we just sit right down
here and have us a little talk.

ANNA. 'Bout what?

KING. Well, just things. Just regular everyday things.
Been out to get the eggs yet this morning?

ANNA. (*exits to kitchen taking gown and RUTH's
coffee cup*) The hen don't lay on Wednesdays.

KING. Oh. It don't?

CLAIRICE. Did you tell Miss Anna about her TV?

KING. That's right. I stopped by the TV World this
morning. They got a special sale on nineteen inch
screens, but I told that boy. We gotta have a twenty-
five. Yes, sir. Twenty-five inches. (*ANNA returns.*)

CLAIRICE. You know, Miss Anna, when you get in
your new house and we have our baby. I can bring him
over sometimes and you can hold him and sing him little
songs. Won't that be nice.

ANNA. Big Jack used to sing to Pearl. "Pretty little
Pearl, Pretty little Pearl. Looks like an angel but she's
my little girl."

CLAIRICE. I don't think we'd want to name our baby
Pearl.

KING. Hadn't picked out a name if it's a girl yet.
Hadn't given it a thought. Anna's a pretty name. We
might even name her Anna.

CLAIRICE. Well, I hope I'll at least be consulted about
what we're going to name the baby I have to suffer to
bring into the world.

KING. Looky here. Here comes Bobby. Right on time. (*BOBBY STACK enters on porch.*) Well, well, here he is now. Hey there, Bobby. We sure do appreciate you coming over here this morning. Sorry about this weather. Lemme get you a cup of coffee. (*exits to kitchen*)

BOBBY. Oh, just a little shower. Morning, Miss Anna.

ANNA. Good morning, Bobby.

BOBBY. Clairice, are you all right?

CLAIRICE. Actually, I'm not doing well at all. I thought I was going into labor last night and King had to rush me to the hospital.

BOBBY. I'm mighty sorry to hear that. You sure you feel up to all this?

CLAIRICE. It was just a false alarm. And I have a duty to be with my husband today. Those flowers you sent to the funeral home (*up, crosses to BOBBY*) were just beautiful, Bobby. I love astors. I think they're one of the best flowers for funerals. They don't wilt so fast. Don't you think so, Miss Anna?

ANNA. Soon as you leave the cemetery, people steal 'em.

CLAIRICE. What?

ANNA. Waste of money to put flowers on a tombstone. There's people just waiting for you to leave so they can come up and steal 'em.

CLAIRICE. Now what kind of people would do that? Steal flowers from the dead?

ANNA. People in a blue truck. I saw 'em waiting at old Nathan's funeral. They'll be there today. You watch.

KING. (*re-entering with coffee*) Clairice, what are you doing out of that wheelchair?

CLAIRICE. I am not a cripple.

KING. Will you please get back in that chair? (*gives BOBBY cup*)

CLAIRICE. I don't see why I have to sit in it all the time. I could sit on the sofa.

KING. (*gets wheelchair*) I'm paying fifteen dollars a week to rent this chair, and I'd appreciate it if you would sit in it as a favor to me.

CLAIRICE. All right. I'm sitting. Are you satisfied?

KING. Thank you. Now. Let's get on with it. Where's Ruth and Raymond?

ANNA. I'll get 'em. (*calling at stairs*) Tabby. John King.

KING. (*to BOBBY*) Nutty as a fruitcake. Just nutty as a fruitcake.

RUTH. (*coming downstairs*) We can't start yet. Raymond's not back.

CLAIRICE. Why, Ruth, what an interesting outfit.

KING. Where's he gone to? He knew we had this meeting.

RUTH. He had something to do.

KING. Well, I'm afraid we'll just have to go ahead and start without him. Bobby here's a busy man, and we got a funeral to go to.

RUTH. He should be back by now. I guess the rain . . .

KING. Can't slow down the legal process, Ruth. Anyway, I think I can speak for Raymond about pertinent matters.

RUTH. No, you cannot speak for Raymond. Bobby, can't we wait just a few more minutes?

BOBBY. Wish I could accommodate you, Ruth. You know I would if I could. But I got to be back at the office before one o'clock. Nothing we're gonna do right now is binding on anybody. I can leave copies of everything and Raymond can look at it.

KING. That's fine. Let's get on with it.

BOBBY. That okay with you, Ruth?

RUTH. Go ahead.

BOBBY. All right. Then let's begin. Contrary to what you might think from watching television shows, a will is not a very interesting document to hear read out loud. So I've taken the liberty of summarizing all the relevant parts. That agreeable to everybody?

KING. Sounds good to me. Just give it to us in plain ordinary English.

BOBBY. Ruth?

RUTH. Whatever Anna wants.

ANNA. I know what it says already. Don't matter to me what he reads.

KING. Maybe you do and maybe you don't. Go ahead, Bobby.

BOBBY. Fine then. I'll proceed. What we have here actually are two wills. One by Pearl Marguerite Vaughnum and one by your grandaddy, John King Vaughnum.

KING. I still don't understand what Big Jack's will's got to do with anything. The place belonged to Aunt Pearl, didn't it?

BOBBY. Well, yes and no. Big Jack left it to his natural children in what's called a life estate.

KING. A life estate. (*Rain and thunder stop.*)

BOBBY. That means that it belongs to them during their lifetime, but they can't dispose of it in any way. His will says that at the death of the last of the natural children, the estate passes to the grandchildren. Any of the grandchildren who want to live on the place permanently get to keep it. If none of them want to live here, the executor . . . Uh, Ruth, who's the oldest, you or Raymond?

RUTH. I am.

BOBBY. Okay, then Ruth's the executrix. The executrix decides how the property is to be disposed of and divides the proceeds in equal parts among the grand-children.

KING. Wait a minute. The will don't name Anna by name? It just says natural children?

BOBBY. That's right.

KING. Well, then, this was all a big hoopla over nothing. The place belongs to us just like I thought.

ANNA. Belongs to me. I am a natural child.

KING. She can't prove she's his daughter. There ain't no proof of that.

ANNA. I am a natural child. It's mine. The will says it's mine. One of the meanings of bastard is natural child. You can look it up right there for yourself.

BOBBY. There's more. I'm not through yet.

KING. We've heard all we need to hear. If there isn't any of Big Jack's children living, then the property goes to the three grandchildren. Right, Bobby? It don't say nothing about Annabel Lee, and it don't say nothing about bastards.

RUTH. It says natural children.

KING. The law don't hold with bastards, does it, Bobby.

BOBBY. Well, if you . . .

RUTH. How does the law hold with bastards in this state? If Annabel Lee is the acknowledged illegitimate daughter of our grandfather, then is she legally entitled to the property?

KING. But she ain't. Who acknowledges her? Just cause people like to gossip don't mean nothing. Talk don't make it true.

ANNA. You know I am.

KING. I don't know nothing of the kind.

RUTH. We all know it. I can't believe you're trying to pull this, King.

CLAIRICE. King is just trying to abide by the law,

aren't you, Honey.

KING. The law's the law, Ruth. Feelings don't count.

RUTH. What would constitute acknowledgement of Miss Anna as the rightful heir?

BOBBY. Well, if Big Jack had publicly acknowledged her as his daughter . . .

RUTH. He as good as did. He knew everybody thought she was his daughter, and he never said any different.

KING. But Big Jack's not here to say that. It's too late. He can't acknowledge nothing if he's dead.

RUTH. How else could we prove it?

BOBBY. If there was a witness to her birth or someone who could testify that . . .

KING. There ain't none. They're all dead. Everybody that counts is dead.

RUTH. What if two of the three grandchildren were willing to say that they knew Anna was the natural daughter of Big Jack? Would that satisfy the spirit of the will?

KING. You're talking perjury here, Ruth.

RUTH. King, will you shut up. Would that be enough, Bobby? If Raymond and I said we knew Anna was Big Jack's daughter? Would that make the property hers?

KING. You don't know nothing of the kind. (*sound of the motorcycle outside*)   SQ 16

RUTH. It's Raymond. Don't anybody say another word until Raymond gets in here. (*RUTH goes to the door as RAYMOND comes up on the porch. He takes off the helmet and shakes rain off his slicker.*)

KING. It don't matter what Raymond says. I can tell you right now, you wouldn't stand a Chinaman's chance in a court of law. Isn't that right, Bobby?

BOBBY. Legally, it's not likely . . .

RUTH. Did you find anything?

KING. We went ahead and started without you, Ray, and it turns out the will doesn't leave the property to Miss Anna after all. That was just an old woman's interpretation of the wording. The property belongs to us cousins just like I expected.

RUTH. Raymond, what took you so long? Was there a birth certificate?

KING. What do you mean? There ain't no birth certificate.

RAYMOND. It wasn't what we thought.

RUTH. Did you find one or not?

RAYMOND. Ruth, I need to talk to you. (*enters house, RUTH follows*)

KING. Now's not the time for secrets. And there ain't no birth certificate.

RUTH. Did you find one?

RAYMOND. Yes.

RUTH. Well?

RAYMOND. (*pulls out a piece of paper from his pocket, crosses to ANNA*) The records show that on December 18, 1909 . . . a midwife by the name of Charity Nunn assisted at the birth of a female child named Annabel Lee. No father's name was recorded. The mother was Beulah Ruth Samuels. (*silence*)

ANNA. Miss Beulah was my mama?

RAYMOND. Yes, mam.

ANNA. I wasn't Big Jack's bastard?

CLAIRICE. Oh my Lord.

ANNA. She never told me.

RUTH. Anna . . .

ANNA. I was her little girl.

KING. Jesus Christ. (*crosses to CLAIRICE, sits on sofa*)

CLAIRICE. Do you realize what this means to our baby? Our poor little unborn baby?

RUTH. What difference does it make now? Nothing's really changed.

KING. Nothing's changed! Everything's changed. Our past is not what we thought it was.

RUTH. Miss Anna's our aunt. We've always known that.

KING. Wait a minute. (*up*) The will says she has to be Big Jack's daughter. It don't count if she's Miss Beulah's. Is that right, Bobby?

BOBBY. Eh, that's right. The property would not go to Miss Beulah's, eh . . . natural child.

RUTH. This is ridiculous. Raymond.

RAYMOND. He's right, Ruth. (*exits to porch*)

RUTH. Anna, I'm sorry. I wanted it to belong to you.

BOBBY. There is one more item. Miss Pearl left her bank account which has a balance of twenty-seven thousand dollars to Annabel Lee. She names her specifically by name.

KING. Well, good. Isn't that nice, Miss Anna. That's a whole lota money. That's enough to take care of you real good. Aunt Pearl's provided for you after all. Well, thank you, Bobby. We sure appreciate your time. I got a little business to take care of with my cousins now, and then we all got to get on out to the cemetery.

BOBBY. Ruth, will you still be here tonight?

RUTH. Yes.

BOBBY. I thought maybe we could . . .

RUTH. Not tonight.

BOBBY. Well, nice seeing you, Raymond.

KING. (*seeing BOBBY out the front door*) Eh, Bob, I know we can count on you to keep our little secret here. After all, you just might be part of this family one of these days.

BOBBY. You can count on me, King. My lips are sealed. (*exits*)

KING. Good. Watch your step there, now. Don't want any lawsuits now that we own the property. Ha ha. (*ANNA moves out into the yard.*)

ANNA. (*looking upward*) Miss Beulah. I was your little girl, Mama. I had a right to know. Mama, it's me, Anna. It's me. I know you loved me. I wish you'd told me so I could have loved you back. I'll love you now, Mama. Mama. You were always so sweet to me. Why didn't you tell me, Mama?

RAYMOND. (*crosses down behind ANNA and places his hands on her shoulders*) It's all right, Miss Anna. Don't cry.

ANNA. I'm crying for joy, Honey. For joy and for sorrow. I was cared about. She was afraid to tell me, but she loved me and wanted me close. (*ANNA enters the house and goes toward the casket.*) She was my mama too. She loved me too, Pearl. Much as she loved you. (*opens casket*) Gimme that ring. (*ANNA pulls the ring off Pearl's finger and slams the lid down. She speaks now as SHARON ROSE.*) I will rise now and go about the city in the streets and in the squares. I will seek him whom my soul loves. I held him and would not let him go until I had brought him into my mother's house. (*ANNA mounts the stairs and continues speaking as she disappears upstairs. Her speech overlaps with CLAIRICE and KING's following dialogue.*) I adjure you, O daughters of Jerusalem by the gazelles or the hinds in the field. Behold, it is the litter of Solomon.

CLAIRICE. Oh, this is more than I can bear.

KING. Honey, I think you better go on home. This has all been too much for you.

CLAIRICE. But what about the funeral?

KING. I'm sure everybody will understand. We got the living to think about, don't we. Now come on. Y'all, I'll be right back in a minute. (*KING pushes CLAIRICE in the wheelchair out the door and off.*)

RAYMOND. Ruth?

RUTH. Our past isn't what we thought it was, is it?

RAYMOND. No.

RUTH. How did she manage that?

RAYMOND. I don't know. We won't ever know, will we? But she did do it. What Beulah wanted was to have her daughter with her, no matter how, and she found a way. And nobody ever knew.

RUTH. Do you think he knew?

RAYMOND. Big Jack? I don't know. It's possible. He loved his wife. She loved her child. Maybe he did know.

RUTH. Isn't it strange. These things happened. Actually happened. In time, in this house. With people we knew, or thought we knew. Can you imagine living with a secret like that your whole life?

RAYMOND. If what you wanted was important enough and keeping it a secret was the only way you could have it. I can imagine it. I think I could do it. Could you?

RUTH. Keep a secret like Miss Beulah's?

RAYMOND. Keep a secret like ours.

RUTH. It's hardly something I'm going to tell the world about.

RAYMOND. I don't mean just keep it. I mean live it. From now on. For the rest of our lives.

RUTH. Here?

RAYMOND. Uh huh. Coming back from Sparta, I knew. I was coming home. I want to feel what Anna feels now. I love you, and I want you close. Like Miss Beulah loved Anna and wanted her close. We'll live here together. You and me and Annabel Lee.

RUTH. We can't do that. People would . . .

RAYMOND. People won't think a thing. Except that a

middle-aged brother and sister came home to fix up the old place and take care of the woman who raised them. You'll ride your motorcycle over to Sparta every day and teach the kids about poetry while Anna and I start hammering and painting. In the fall when the leaves turn we'll drive up in the mountains, and at Christmas we'll chop down the biggest evergreen on the place and put it over there next to the piano. On Saturday nights we'll go to the movies, and one Sunday a month we'll have our cousins King and Clairice and all their children over for fried chicken and eggs goldenrod. Nobody will ever know, Ruth. There won't even be a record anywhere for someone to find a hundred years from now saying Ruth and Raymond Brown loved and needed each other all their lives, and finally came home to live the way their hearts told them.

RUTH. Raymond.

RAYMOND. This is it, Ruth. This is where the home stretch starts. Right here at Honeysuckle Hill.

ANNA. (*from upstairs*) I am black, but comely, O ye daughters of Jerusalem.

RAYMOND. We'll take care of her. We'll keep her here and let her spend the rest of her days thinking about her mother. That's all she cares about now.

RUTH. She's got good reason to be angry, you know.

RAYMOND. It's what she's got. And this is what we've got. It's our chance, Ruth.

ANNA. (*entering from the landing holding small locket on gold chain*) See this? She gave it to me. Told me not to show it to anybody. Not even Pearl. It's got her picture in it. See. When she was young. You think I favor her?

RAYMOND. Ruth?

ANNA. I have her locket and her ring. I am bejeweled. Bejeweled.

RUTH. All right.

RAYMOND. You will? You will? Okay. Now. When King comes back . . .

ANNA. I am the Rose of Sharon, the lily of the valley.

RAYMOND. Anna, about the property. This is what we're going to do . . .

ANNA. If it had been my mother's house, she would have left it to me. But her husband left it to his children, and I'm not one of his. Beulah was my mother, and my father was King Solomon.

RUTH. Listen, Anna. You can stay here. We've got it all figured out. Raymond and I are going to come here and live with you.

ANNA. No.

RUTH. But you said you wanted to . . .

ANNA. I said I wanted to live in this house and die in it. Owning it. If it's not mine, I'm not staying. Annabel Lee is through living in somebody else's house.

RAYMOND. What difference does it make who owns it? We'll all three live here.

ANNA. Uh uh.

RUTH. Anna, what's wrong with you?

ANNA. It was wrong of my mother to bring me here SQ 1 and make me grow up not knowing who I was and not having anybody like me to be close to. And it was wrong of her not to tell me she was my mother. I wouldn't have told anybody. But I believe that she loved me. And I forgive her.

RAYMOND. You want to see a shopping center named after her?

RUTH. Raymond, leave her alone.

RAYMOND. Is that the way you want your mother remembered? As the Beulah Land Shopping Mall? (*sound of car door slamming*)

ANNA. Here he comes just bouncing like a bullfrog. (*pause*) You want to sell it?

RAYMOND. To you?

ANNA. I'll give you twenty-seven thousand dollars for it.

RAYMOND. You want to buy your own home?

ANNA. Not mine unless you sell it to me.

RAYMOND. (*to RUTH*) Can we do that?

RUTH. Of course we can. I'm the executrix. We can sell it to whomever I say, and I say we sell it to Annabel Lee.

RAYMOND. King's gonna love this.

RUTH. He'll get his third, just like the will says.

ANNA. I'll let you two live here with me, and when I die, I'll leave it to you in my will.

RAYMOND. Sold. You have just bought yourself a fine piece of real estate.

RUTH. Be sure to name us by name in that will.

KING. (*returning in a hurry*) Well, cousins, this is one day we're not likely to soon forget. But life goes on, don't it? And we gotta go on with it. Miss Anna, I want you to know that what happened today don't change our feelings toward you. You couldn't help how you got born, and we don't blame you for it. You can count on Clairice and me. Course you won't probably need any of our help since Aunt Pearl was so generous to leave you her savings account. You just take your time getting your things ready, and Friday, I'll drive you over to Berry Hill just like I promised.

ANNA. I'm not going to Berry Hill.

KING. Well, I don't think Aunt Pearl's savings account will be enough to buy the place we were talking about.

ANNA. Not going anywhere. I'm staying right here in

my mama's house.

KING. This is not . . . your mama's house. And you cannot stay here. Ruth, would you please get her to listen to reason.

RUTH. Me?

KING. Raymond, I know you got a plane to catch.

RAYMOND. Yes, I do, but as soon as I can get things wrapped up in New York, I'm coming back to stay.

KING. Here? For good?

RAYMOND. That's right.

KING. Well. Well good. Be mighty nice to have you home. Clairice'll be tickled. You oughta take a look at that little house on Pike Street, yourself. It's nothing fancy, but you could fix it up to suit you. Put in a barbecue grill and a jacuzzi.

RUTH. A jacuzzi. That's a good idea.

KING. Yeah.

RAYMOND. (to RUTH) Right next to the smoke house?

KING. Wait a minute. You're not thinking about living here?

RAYMOND. Yes. I am.

KING. But you can't. I mean, why would you want to live in this old place?

RAYMOND. It's our heritage.

KING. Heritage hell. It's falling down rotten. Raymond, you know I got plans for this place. Dreams. I'm talking about the future.

RAYMOND. So am I. I'm sorry, King. You're just going to have to dream yourself up another dream. My wandering days are over. I'm coming home to live at Honeysuckle Hill. And Miss Annabel Lee is going to be the lady of the manor, aren't you, Anna. We're going to fix this place up and put some real chickens out there in that hen house. I tell you, King boy, I may even buy me a mule and plow an get out there and turn up some of that good Vaughnum earth.

KING. Why you son of a bitch. You just want the place for yourself.

RAYMOND. Indeed I do, cousin. Indeed I do.

KING. Ruth, are you a party to this?

RAYMOND. Ruth and I are going to grow old in the house where we were children.

KING. Well, that's the goddammedest arrangement I ever heard.

RAYMOND. It's an arrangement in keeping with our heritage and our way of life, King. Bachelor brother and spinster sister share the old family home and take care of their elderly aunt. What could be more Southern and respectable?

KING. Respectable my ass. You just want to get your hands on this property. Yesterday you couldn't get rid of this place fast enough.

RAYMOND. We had a change of heart. Tell Clairice I'm going to write a book about "All Our Yesterdays." I'll autograph the first copy for her.

RUTH. I may even write a book about Sharon Rose.

ANNA. You can write what you want to. And if you're dead set on getting chickens, then get 'em. But don't expect me to take care of them.

RAYMOND. Here comes Mr. Sammons. Time to get on down to the cemetery. Everybody ready?

RUTH. Wait a minute, let me get my fox.

ANNA. I'm gon' show y'all that truck where the people wait to steal the flowers.

RAYMOND. (*as he, RUTH, and ANNA go out the door*) Your taxi cab's waiting, King.

KING. You go off for twenty years and then come

home and expect to take up where you left off. It don't work that way, fella. You can't hang on to the past. Things change, and we gotta move with the times. You gotta believe in your dreams and be willing to . . .

RUTH. (*offstage*) You coming, King?

KING. Who am I talking to? I'm standing here talking to a dead body. You hateful old woman. I never liked you. (*KING goes out the front door.*) Miss Anna, why don't you ride up front with me? (*KING goes on down the steps and down the sidewalk as lights fade to black.*)

BLACKOUT

THE END

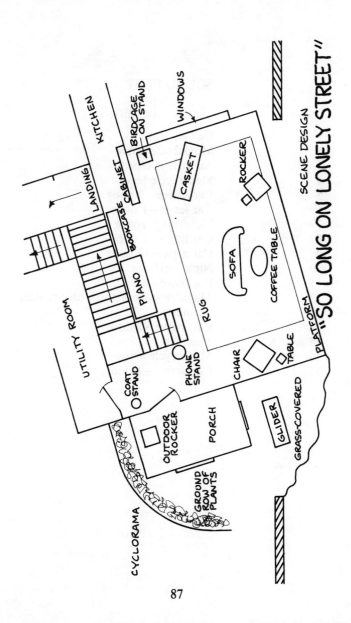

CYCLORAMA

UTILITY ROOM

LANDING

KITCHEN

BIRDCAGE ON STAND

WINDOWS

COAT STAND

PIANO

BOOKCASE CABINET

CASKET

PHONE STAND

ROCKER

OUTDOOR ROCKER

RUG

SOFA

GROUND ROW OF PLANTS

PORCH

CHAIR

TABLE

COFFEE TABLE

GLIDER

GRASS-COVERED

PLATFORM

SCENE DESIGN

"SO LONG ON LONELY STREET"

SOUND PLOT

Cue #	Effect
1	Day environs
2	Motorcycle arrive
3	Air rifle if taped
4	Motorcycle leave
5	Car arrive – 2 door
6	Car leave – 1 door
7	Motorcycle arrive
8	Car leave – 2 door
9	Car arrive – 2 door
10	Night environs
11	Car leave – 1 door
12	Thunder storm (storm on cassette)
13	Thunder
14	Car arrive – 2 door
15 & 15A	Thunder
16	Motorcycle arrive
17	Car arrive – 1 door

FURNITURE BREAKDOWN

Front Porch
    Glider, 7'0 × 2'8
    Rocker, 2'3 × 2'6
    Plant on step

Living Room
    Table—oval, 2'5 × 1'6
    Coat rack
    Piano 5'9 × 2'3
    Piano bench
    Electric fan
    Standing lamp
    Chair, 2'9 × 2'9—doilie on back
    Table—square, 2'6 × 1'0
    Mag rack, 1'6 × 1'3
    Sofa, 7'6 × 2'9—3 pillows & afghan
    Table—oval, 1'9 × 2'6
    Rocker, 3'0 × 2'9
    3 × 5 rug
    9 × 12 rug
    4 × 6 rug
    Cabinet

Dining Room
    Coffin, 3'0 × 7'4
    Coffin stand
    6 chairs
    China cabinet, 4'9 × 1'0
    6 × 9 rug

PRESET

Garment bag
Sealed bottle of sherry in brown paper bag
Sunglasses
Motorcycle helmet
Pack of Merit Ultra Lights w/5–7 cigarettes
Bic Lighter
Funeral parlor stand pre. w/ light 'on' & cord coiled
    inside
Gold Cross pen
Guest book
Straw purse w/ compact, lipgloss, brush, & hanky
Box of chicken
6 Pack of Coke
Bag w/ 1 box of "okra", 2 large containers of cole slaw,
    1 container w/ 2 Jalapeño peppers
Briefcase w/Jack's will, Pearl's will & summary paper
    clipped together
Spray bottle of water
Birth certificate
Wheelchair

Utility Room

Ironing board
Pearl's dress (set on ironing board)

S.L.

Brush w/gray hairs
BB gun
Guitar

Pitcher of iced tea filled to bottom of band
Tray & 4 iced tea glasses w/ice, mint, & lemon circles
2 glasses w/ice & 1″ of vodka
3 Glasses—2 w/ ice and 1 w/o & 1″ of vodka
Open bag of Lays potato chips
6 Eggs
Roll of paper towels (1 loose)
Damp sponge
Plate of Eggs Goldenrod
Bottle of vodka 1/2 full
2 Empty glasses
2 Cups of coffee 1/2 full
Ashtray w/water
Locket
Iron
Sprinkler bottle
Wedding ring

Onstage

Phone Table:
Phone (set facing DS.)
Wastebasket DS.

Piano:
Fan (plugged in)
Ashtray w/sand

Bookcase:
Dictionary
3 Volumes of poetry

Cabinet:
3 Sherry glasses
5 Napkins prefolded
4 Plates

5 Forks
3 Serving spoons

Left End Table:
Anna's glasses (top shelf)
Sewing kit w/top loose & threaded needle (2nd shelf)
Ashtray w/water

Right End Table:
Ashtray w/water

Trunk Preset:
Shoes — Ruth 40's
Suit — Ruth 40's
Fox
Pink peignoir
Veil
Mirror & brush
Fan
Military hat
Bronze shoes
Flag
Spool necklace
Packet of letters
Will
Doll

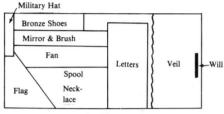

Top View

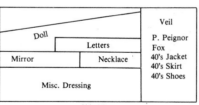

Side View

Doors:
Front door open
Screen door closed
Kitchen door open
Utility door closed

Coffin:
Pearl in nightgown
Extra ring
Coffin closed

Notes:

Instant iced tea is used for the iced tea.
Water is used for the vodka.
Eggs Goldenrod is a piece of toast w/peach yogurt on
  top.
Coffee is flat coke.

Consumables per show:

  Sherry
  Iced tea
  Lemon circles
  Ice cubes
  Mint sprays
  Large bag of Lays potato chips
  2 Eggs – broken
  4 Eggs – not broken
  Wash & dry packets
  Classic Coke
  Chicken
  Coleslaw
  Mashed potatoes
  Gravy
  Cottage cheese
  Cigarettes
  Candy
  Tums
  Rolls
  Plastic forks
  Paper towels
  Bandaids

5 Practicals:
   Overhead on porch
   Overhead in foyer
   Overhead above coffin
   Standing lamp in living room
   Podium light

HUSBANDRY
(LITTLE THEATRE—DRAMA)

By PATRICK TOVATT

2 men, 2 women—Interior

At its recent world premiere at the famed Actors Theatre of Louisville, this enticing new drama moved an audience of theatre professionals up off their seats and on to their feet to cheer. Mr. Tovatt has given us an insightful drama about what is happening to the small, family farm in America—and what this means for the future of the country. The scene is a farmhouse whose owners are on the verge of losing their farm. They are visited by their son and his wife, who live "only" eight hours' drive away. The son has a good job in the city, and his wife does, too. The son, Harry, is really put on the horns of a dilemma when he realizes that he is his folks' only hope. The old man can't go it alone anymore—and he needs his son. Pulling at him from the other side is his wife, who does not want to leave her job and uproot her family to become a farm wife. *Husbandry*, then, is ultimately about what it means to be a *husband*—both in the farm and in the family sense. *Variety* praised the "delicacy of Tovatt's dialogue", and called the play "a literate exploration of family responsibilities in a mobile society." Said *Time*: "The play simmers so gently for so long, as each potential confrontation is deflected with Chekhovian shrugs and silences, that when it boils into hostility it sears the audience."   (#10169)

(Royalty, $60–$40.)

CLARA'S PLAY
(LITTLE THEATRE—DRAMA)

By JOHN OLIVE

3 men, 1 woman—Exterior

Clara, an aging spinster, lives alone in a remote farmhouse. She is the last surviving member of one of the area's most prominent families. It is summer, 1915. Enter an immigrant, feisty soul named Sverre looking for a few days' work before moving on. But Clara's farm needs more than just a few days' work, and Sverre stays on to help Clara fix up and run the farm. It soon becomes clear unscrupulous local businessmen are bilking Clara out of money and hope to gain control of her property. Sverre agrees to stay on to help Clara keep her family's property. "A story of determination, loyalty. It has more than a measure of love, of resignation, of humor and loyalty."—Chicago Sun-Times. "A playwright of unusual sensitivity in delineating character and exploring human relationships." —Chicago Tribune. "Gracefully-written, with a real sense of place."—Village Voice. A recent success both at Chicago's fine Wisdom Bridge Theatre and at the Great American Play Festival of the world-reknowned Actors Theatre of Louisville; and, on tour, starring Jean Stapleton.   (#5076)

(Royalty, $50–$35.)